TIMEOUT!

HEADS UP, FOOTBALL FANS

HEAD-TO-HEAD FOOTBALL is a unique book; it has two fronts and no back. It is somewhat like two football teams facing each other at the line of scrimmage! Choose the superstar you want to read about first, read his story, then flip the book over and read about the other player.

You'll read how two different players from two different backgrounds ended up in the National Football League. You'll see how they're alike, too. You'll get the inside story of the Dallas Cowboys' Super Bowl-winning super quarterback, Troy Aikman, and the lowdown on the San Francisco 49ers' record-setting quarterback, Steve Young.

After reading both athletes' stories, tackle the amazing center section of the book. It has fantastic photos, complete statistics, and a comic strip, all of which show just how these two quarterbacks stack up against each other.

Okay, it's time for the coin toss. So pick Troy or Steve, and get ready for all the Head-to-Head action!

Head-to-Head Football: Troy Aikman and Steve Young by David Levine and Darice Bailer

A SPORTS ILLUSTRATED FOR KIDS publication/July 1996

SPORTS ILLUSTRATED FOR KIDS and KIDS are registered trademarks of Time Inc.

Cover and interior design by Miriam Dustin
Illustrations by Steve McGarry
Cover photographs by Sportschrome East/West

All rights reserved. Copyright © 1996 Time Inc.

No part of this book may be reproduced or transmitted in any form or by any means, electronic or mechanical, including photocopying, recording, or by any information storage and retrieval system, without permission in writing from the publisher.

For information, write: SPORTS ILLUSTRATED FOR KIDS

Head-to-Head Football: Troy Aikman and Steve Young is published by SPORTS ILLUSTRATED FOR KIDS, a division of Time Inc. Its trademark is registered in the U.S. Patent and Trademark Office and in other countries. SPORTS ILLUSTRATED FOR KIDS, 1271 Avenue of the Americas, New York, New York 10020

ISBN 1-886749-14-0

PRINTED IN THE UNITED STATES OF AMERICA
10 9 8 7 6 5 4 3 2 1

Head-to-Head Football: Troy Aikman and Steve Young is a production of **SPORTS ILLUSTRATED FOR KIDS Books**: Cathrine Wolf, Editorial Director; Margaret Sieck, Senior Editor (Project Editor); Jill Safro, Stephen Thomas, Associate Editors; Sherie Holder, Assistant Editor

Time Inc. New Business Development: David Gitow, Director; Stuart Hotchkiss, Associate Director; Peter Shapiro, Assistant Director; Mary Warner McGrade, Fufillment Director; Robert Fox, John Sandklev, Alicia Wilcox, Development Managers; John Calvano, Editorial Operations Manager; Donna Miano-Ferrara, Production Manager; Tricia Griffin, Financial Manager; Mike Holahan, Daniel Melore, Allison Weiss, Associate Development Managers; Dawn Weland, Assistant Development Manager; Charlotte Siddiqui, Marketing Assistant

HEAD TO HEAD FOOTBALL

TROY AIKMAN

by David Levine

A SPORTS ILLUSTRATED FOR KIDS Book

CONTENTS

1 The 'Boys Are Back 6

2 From City Slicker to Country Boy 13

3 Aikmania! 21

4 Even Cowboys Get the Blues 29

5 March to the Super Bowl 37

6 Repeat! 45

7 Once and Future Champs 52

8 A Shy Superstar 61

   Troy Aikman's Career Stats 64

1

THE 'BOYS ARE BACK

Everything was perfect. The sun was shining. The sky was clear and blue. It was Sunday, January 31, 1993 — Super Bowl Sunday.

The Dallas Cowboys were playing the Buffalo Bills in Super Bowl XXVII. The stands were filled with 98,374 screaming fans. This was the game all football fans had been waiting for.

The game was being played at The Rose Bowl, in Los Angeles, California. Dallas quarterback Troy Aikman knew the field well. Troy had played in this stadium for two years as quarterback of his college team, the University of California at Los Angeles (UCLA) Bruins. He hoped that being familiar with the place would make him less nervous than usual before a big game.

Before every game, Troy gets anxious. He gets butterflies in his stomach, which is normal for anyone who is about to do something challenging, like play in an important game.

But this wasn't just *any* important game. This was

the Super Bowl, the biggest game of the year! For the Cowboys, it was a huge game because they hadn't been in a Super Bowl for 15 years. For Troy, it was easily the biggest game of his life. So you can imagine that he had the biggest butterflies of his life, too. When his name was announced over the stadium loudspeaker and as he ran onto the field, he was an emotional wreck! The butterflies felt like a flock of birds in his gut. He had never felt this nervous before.

Troy told himself to calm down. He had to relax to play well. Troy usually settles down once the game begins. His confidence returns. But this time, it didn't. He felt as if all the fans in the stands and the millions more around the world watching on TV, were staring at *him* (which, of course, they were). He was hyperventilating — breathing so quickly that he almost fainted. The beginning of the game was a big blur.

Because of his nervousness, Troy did not play well early on. Dallas's first two drives went nowhere. Troy was having trouble finding his receivers, the players who are supposed to catch the ball. He completed only three of his first six passes. On one play, Troy could hear running back Emmitt Smith yelling for the ball, but Troy couldn't see Emmitt.

"I was having a tough time getting into the feel of the ball game," Troy admitted later.

Buffalo scored first and led, 7–0. Troy talked with his coaches. They needed to try something new. Buffalo's tough defense was not letting Troy make passes to the outside of the field. To cope with that, the Cowboys would have to throw more to the middle of the field.

When Dallas safety James Washington picked off a pass from Bills quarterback Jim Kelly, Troy and the offense made their move. The team got into its rhythm. So did Troy. He marched the Cowboys on a 47-yard drive toward the end zone. At the Bills' 23-yard line, he spotted tight end Jay Novacek and threw a perfect pass. Touchdown!

"The touchdown to Novacek was the throw that got Troy his rhythm and confidence," Dallas offensive coordinator, Norv Turner, told *Sports Illustrated* after the game. "It had to be perfect. After that I felt that he was going to be fine."

Troy was a lot more than fine. Like the weather, he was nearly perfect the rest of game.

The game stayed close for a while. After Dallas returned a Buffalo fumble for a touchdown, the Cowboys led, 14–7. Later, when Buffalo kicked a field goal, the Bills were trailing by only 4 points, 14–10.

After the kickoff, the Cowboys got the ball at their own 28-yard line. Troy took his team 72 yards in only five plays. From the Bills' 19-yard line, Troy threw a touchdown pass to Cowboy receiver Michael Irvin. Dallas now led, 21–10.

The Bills fumbled on their next possession, and Dallas recovered. With the ball on Buffalo's 18, Michael was open again, and Troy threw. Another score! Troy now had three touchdown passes before the half had ended! The Cowboys were ahead, 28–10.

In the second half, Dallas put Buffalo away. Troy's 45-yard bomb to wide receiver Alvin Harper was his fourth touchdown pass of the game. The final score was 52–17. The Dallas Cowboys had won their first world championship in 15 years. It was one of the most lopsided victories in Super Bowl history.

Much of the credit for Dallas's victory went to the defense, which returned two fumbles for touchdowns. Troy himself was impressed. *Sports Illustrated* reported that Troy told his coach, Jimmy Johnson, "I've never seen a defensive performance like that in my entire life. Just awesome!"

Even so, there was one true star of this game. After that shaky start, Troy completed 11 of his next 13 passes in the first half. In the second half, he was 8-of-11. His final numbers were 22-of-30 passes completed for 273 yards. He threw no interceptions. And don't forget those four TDs.

When it came time to vote for the Super Bowl Most Valuable Player (MVP), it was no contest. Troy won easily. At the age of 26, he was the youngest MVP since Joe Montana, the great quarterback of the San Francisco 49ers. Joe had won the MVP award in 1982 when he was 25.

Troy smashed one of Joe's records. In the 1989–90

playoffs, Joe had thrown a record-setting 83 passes in three games without an interception. In the playoffs of 1992–93, the Cowboys had played three games and Troy had thrown a total of 89 passes. Not one had been picked off.

Joe Montana is considered the quarterback of the 1980's. These days, Troy is being called the quarterback of the nineties. When the Cowboys won Super Bowl XXX, in January 1996, Troy collected his third NFL championship ring. Troy now owns as many Super Bowl rings as Joe does. (Only Terry Bradshaw has more. Terry won four Super Bowls with the Pittsburgh Steelers in the seventies.)

It really isn't fair to compare Troy and Joe. They are different types of quarterback. Troy is bigger than Joe. His arm is much stronger. Troy's style is more aggressive and determined. Troy always looks as if he's giving it everything he's got. Joe was known as one of the smartest quarterbacks in history. He made everything look easy, and it always seemed as though he weren't even trying hard. Joe always played hard, of course. It just didn't appear that way.

Troy reminds a lot of people of quarterbacks from earlier eras. Former Cowboy Cliff Harris, who played on Dallas's two Super Bowl champions in the 1970's, told *Sports Illustrated:* "You see a lot of the top quarterbacks of today and you get the feeling that their minds aren't completely into it. Troy's not like that. He's old world, Billy Kilmer, Roger Staubach, that kind of quarterback."

Being compared to Roger must have made Troy proud. Roger was the star quarterback of the great Cowboy teams in the 1970's. He also happened to be one of Troy's idols. As a boy growing up in a part of Oklahoma not far from Dallas, Texas, Troy had been a rabid Cowboy fan. Roger was his favorite player.

Early in his pro career, Troy had been compared to Roger — not always favorably. In Troy's first few seasons, the Cowboys were not good. It's difficult to play well on a bad team. Playing on a good team makes everyone play better. The quarterback has more protection from his offensive line. He has better receivers and runners to give the ball to. But not on a poor team. Because the Cowboys were terrible back then, Troy had no chance to perform as well as Roger had. As a result, Troy took a lot of heat.

But the young quarterback was patient. He took the criticism in stride. "Every quarterback in this league has something that is not right with his situation," Troy said later. "Steve Young has to battle the legend of Joe Montana. I have to face Roger Staubach's accomplishments. I've gone through tough times. But everybody has. People have this misconception that everything has been handed to me on a silver spoon. Nothing is given to anybody in life."

Troy waited for better days. By his fourth season, that patience finally paid off. The Cowboys had become the best team in football. Troy Aikman was, arguably, the best player on the best team. What a feeling!

12 TROY AIKMAN

After Troy's first Super Bowl, a reporter asked him if this had been the best moment of his career. "I have a real hard time classifying anything as my biggest moment, my favorite color, or whatever," Troy answered. "I'd have to say, though, that the Super Bowl was [my] greatest moment in sports."

FROM CITY SLICKER TO COUNTRY BOY

Troy Kenneth Aikman was born on November 21, 1966, in West Covina, California. He was born about two months before the first Super Bowl was played. He grew up in Cerritos, which is a suburb of Los Angeles. His parents, Kenneth and Charlyn, had three children. Troy is the youngest. His older sisters are named Terri and Tammi.

Troy was born with a physical problem. Both of his feet grew crookedly. His legs bowed slightly below his knees. His toes curled under his feet. It is similar to a condition called "club feet."

Troy's doctor put casts on both his legs when Troy was less than 1 year old. The casts were changed every two weeks. When he started to learn to walk, Troy had to wear special shoes. They looked like regular shoes, except that the toes pointed away from each other. To others, it looked as if he were wearing his shoes on the wrong feet.

He wore these shoes until he was 3. When Troy went

to bed, the heels of the shoes were strapped together. All of this was done to help his feet and legs grow properly. It was uncomfortable, but it paid off. His problem was corrected. As a young boy, he could run and play just like the other kids.

Having gone through all this at an early age, Troy showed he could be tough. He thinks the toughness comes from his father, Kenneth. Mr. Aikman was a construction worker and pipe layer. A pipe layer puts the pipes that carry gas or water into the ground. Troy once said that his toughness comes "from back when I was younger and seeing how hard my dad worked and how tough he was and wanting to prove to him that I was tough, too."

Troy always loved sports. He played hoops with his older sisters in their driveway. They rode bikes to a park and played touch football. His sister Terri would play quarterback. She could throw better than he could!

As a kid, Troy dreamed of playing in the pros someday — pro baseball, that is. At age 10, he began practicing his signature for autographs! "I told my mom that one day someone was going to want my autograph and I needed to have it down," he said.

Troy clearly had a lot of confidence in himself. Sometimes, however, a confident person can become a cocky person. Troy could be a bad sport at times. He even yelled at his baseball coach one day. The coach had called a timeout and put a new player in at second base. Troy was the shortstop. He thought the new player was no good. He started screaming at the coach, saying that the kid shouldn't be in the game.

Later in that game, Troy made a great catch. His teammates carried him off the field as a hero. But his mom had other ideas. She came down from the stands and approached her son. She grabbed Troy by the shirt and dragged him to their car.

She yelled: "If you ever do that again, I will pull you off the field and that will be the end of sports."

"My mom chewed me out," Troy remembered. "She told me how embarrassed she was that I would be so ugly out on the field." He learned his lesson well.

"I learned behavior is one thing I could change," Troy stated in a book about his life he wrote with Greg Brown called *Things Change*. "[After that incident,] I never bad-mouthed another player."

Troy loved living in California. He could play sports all year long. He loved baseball and football. He had lots of friends to play with, and he liked living near Los Angeles. As you might imagine, he was shocked when his family moved to Oklahoma.

Troy was 12 years old. His dad bought a ranch in the small town of Henryetta. Henryetta is about 200 miles north of Dallas, Texas. It had a population of only 6,000 people. Cerritos, where the Aikmans had been living, had

50,000 people. Nearby Los Angeles had several million!

After he moved, Troy felt culture shock, which means he had a difficult time adjusting to the differences between the two places. In Cerritos, there were many kids in the neighborhood. In Henryetta, the Aikmans had no neighbors close by. In California, Troy could ride his bike to a mall or to a McDonald's. Henryetta was so small, it had no McDonald's! "I didn't like Oklahoma at all," he recalls. Plus, it was cold! "It was like, 'Man, where's the beach?'" he says.

The ranch Troy moved to had 172 acres. An acre is about the size of one football field. That's 172 football fields for Troy to play on.

Unfortunately, Troy didn't have much time to play. They raised cattle, pigs, and chickens on the ranch. Troy had to help with the chores before and after school. He especially hated having to feed the pigs before school every morning. The farm was different from the suburbs!

Moving is very difficult for any family. Troy wondered how his parents could just move like that, changing their

HEAD TO HEAD

Troy grew up on a ranch and likes country life. But he's a Cowboy, not a cowboy. He says he can't even ride a horse!

lives so much. He was angry at his parents for a while.

But in time, Troy grew to love Oklahoma. He liked the values of the people. They were friendly, courteous, and helpful to one another. "I identified with the people so well, that type of lifestyle," Troy says. "The laid-back, easy-going people. I enjoyed everything about growing up in a small town in rural America." He also learned to love country music.

One other thing he especially loved: Football. People in Oklahoma are crazy about football. In particular, they love the University of Oklahoma Sooners and the Dallas Cowboys. Like most kids in Oklahoma, Troy dreamed that someday he would play for both those teams. Sometimes, dreams come true!

When Troy started playing organized football, he was a quarterback. In junior high, however, he decided to try a new position — fullback. He soon discovered that blocking and being tackled weren't for him. He thought about quitting, but his dad wouldn't let him. Troy stuck it out, but he went back to playing quarterback the next season.

In high school, Troy played football, baseball, and basketball. He was so good at baseball, college scouts came to watch him pitch. Even the major league teams were interested. In his senior year, a scout for the New York Mets called. It was the night before baseball's amateur draft, when pro teams pick young players and try to sign them to professional contracts. The scout asked Troy if he would be interested in signing a contract and how much money he would want. In *Things Change,* Troy wrote that only a few years earlier, he would have played baseball for free. But his dreams had changed. His favorite sport was no longer baseball: It was football.

He went ahead and told the scout he would probably sign for $200,000, which was a big signing bonus. He felt it scared the team away!

Troy played on his high school football team for each of his four years in school. The Henryetta school teams were called the Fighting Hens. The Hens did fight hard, but they didn't succeed. They lost most of their games while Troy was there.

To make things worse, the players were teased about the unusual nickname. Opposing fans laughed and threw rubber chickens onto the field at their games against the Hens!

Troy was a standout, though. In one game, Troy made a spectacular touchdown pass that almost won the game for Henryetta. After the game, the opposing coach told him, "We'll be watching you someday on Monday Night Football." The coach knew he had seen someone special that day.

High school quarterbacks are often confident and popular students. Troy might have been the quarterback of the school team, but he thought of himself as a "real dorky kid." His nickname at the time was "Ears," because his ears stuck out so far from his head. Troy was known as a quiet, polite kid.

In school, his best class was typing. His high school principal, Rick Enis, remembers Troy competing in a typing contest against 38 girls. "At lunch assembly, they announced the third-place winner, some little girl," says Mr. Enis. "The second-place winner was a little girl, and then the winner was . . . Troy! I kind of dropped my fork, although it was kind of embarrassing for him."

It might have been embarrassing, but it certainly helped him later in his life. In college, he used his typing skills to earn money. He typed term papers for his classmates.

Fortunately or unfortunately, there is no pro typing league. Therefore, Troy concentrated on football. Several colleges wanted Troy to play for their teams. Troy wanted to stay in Oklahoma. The two big schools there are the University of Oklahoma and Oklahoma State. They both wanted Troy. Soon, they began a recruiting war to get him.

The head coach at Oklahoma State was Jimmy Johnson — the same Jimmy Johnson who later would coach Troy on the Cowboys. The head coach at the University of Oklahoma was Barry Switzer. He is now the Cowboys' coach.

Troy first met Jimmy Johnson when Troy was a sophomore in high school. He liked Mr. Johnson right away, and told him he would play for Oklahoma State after he graduated.

But by the time he was a high school senior, Troy had changed his mind. Coach Switzer promised Troy that he would design his offense around Troy if he would come to Oklahoma. Troy could become a star there. That was all Troy needed to hear. He decided to play for Barry Switzer and the Oklahoma Sooners.

AIKMANIA!

For many years, the Oklahoma Sooners have been one of the best teams in college football. Coach Switzer was part of that tradition. The Sooners were contenders for a national championship when Troy became their quarterback in 1984.

For years, Oklahoma had used what is called a wishbone offense. In this offense, two running backs stand behind and to either side of the quarterback, in a *Y* shape. As a group, the three look like the wishbone of a turkey. The wishbone offense requires a quarterback who can run. He is treated almost as a third running back. He must be able to run *and* to pass, but passing is not as important. Troy was not a great runner. He was a great passer. So it was important that Oklahoma change its offense for him.

There was another reason Troy chose Oklahoma. Oklahoma had also recruited a running back named Marcus Dupree. Marcus was as highly sought after as Troy. He was probably the best runner in the country. Coach Switzer thought Marcus would be better in an I-formation. In that formation, the running backs stand in a line behind the quarterback, like the letter *I*. The I-formation is the more typical offense people use passes from — just what Troy was looking for. It seemed perfect for everyone.

But early in the school year, before the team started playing its games, Marcus dropped out of college. Without his star runner, Coach Switzer decided to go back to the wishbone. Troy was stuck. He was disappointed in Coach Switzer. He told a newspaper reporter later that Coach Switzer "lied to me, no question about that, when he recruited me. He tells me he's going to a passing game, and four days into workouts, he's back to the wishbone."

But Troy's anger at his coach didn't last. "I will say this for the man — he was very up front about everything after that," Troy admitted. "I liked him, actually. Still do."

Troy tried to stick it out at Oklahoma. His freshman year he played in only three games. He spent most of the season watching his older teammates and learning about college football. When he did play, he struggled. He started one game, against the University of Kansas. He was the first freshman quarterback to start a game for the Sooners in almost 40 years!

It showed. Troy completed only two of 14 passes, for a measly eight yards. He had three passes picked off — one for a touchdown. Oklahoma lost, 28–11.

Troy wasn't expected to be great as a freshman. But big things *were* expected of him his sophomore year. He now had a year of experience. He also had grown to 6' 3", and he weighed more than 200 pounds. That is a good size for a fullback, who plays a much more physical position than a quarterback! A quarterback Troy's size, with his talent, is often called a "can't miss" prospect — he can't miss being a great player. Even though Troy wasn't a great runner, Coach Switzer still thought he could run the wishbone and lead the Sooners to a national championship.

The team was ranked Number 1 at the start of the season. With Troy at quarterback, the Sooners won their first three games. But Troy was struggling with the wishbone. In their fourth game, Oklahoma played its toughest opponent of the season — the University of Miami Hurricanes.

The Hurricanes were then coached by none other than Jimmy Johnson. (Remember him from Oklahoma State?) They had a high-scoring offense and a powerful defense.

But the Sooners were ready. Troy was inspired to play his best game ever. He completed his first six passes, one of which went for a touchdown. His seventh was nearly a completion. Only a great defensive play knocked the ball away from his receiver. But that was the last pass Troy would throw that day — and that season.

On the next play, Troy was sacked hard. He was crushed to the ground, and he couldn't get up. His left ankle was broken. Troy was carried off the field. His season was over.

Oklahoma lost that game to Miami, 27–14. What would the Sooners do now, without Troy? Many fans expected the worst. But Troy's backup, Jamelle Holieway, was a fine quarterback and a better runner than Troy. He was better qualified for the wishbone offense than Troy was. In fact, with Jamelle at quarterback, the Sooners won the national championship. They beat Penn State, 25–10, in the Orange Bowl that year to clinch the title.

Troy was left confused. If he stayed at Oklahoma, he might not play. Jamelle was better for the offense Oklahoma was using. Still, Troy knew he could be a great quarterback. He just needed to go to a school that would let him play his game. He decided to transfer to a new school.

Troy told Coach Switzer about his decision. The coach understood completely. "He was as happy as a coach can possibly be the day I told him I was transferring," Troy commented. Now Troy had another problem. Where would he go?

Coach Switzer promised to help Troy find a good school. One of the first to be interested was the University of Miami. Coach Jimmy Johnson *still* wanted Troy to be his quarterback. And once again, Troy told him no! (You have to give Coach Johnson credit: He kept trying!) Troy decided he didn't like the city of Miami or the environment of the school. "Those kind of things mean a lot to me," he said.

Troy finally decided on UCLA. Coach Switzer told him it would be a great place for him to play. UCLA played the kind of offense Troy liked. It's called a pro-style offense. That means it is a lot like the offenses used by most professional teams. This offense features long and short passes mixed with a strong running game. Here, Troy could learn the pro style, which would make him even more valuable after he graduated.

Troy liked the head coach at UCLA, Terry Donahue. They became close friends. Troy felt that Coach Donahue really cared about Troy as a person, not just as a quarterback. That made Troy feel comfortable at UCLA.

He also liked the school because he had lived in Los Angeles as a young boy. He felt comfortable in the city right away. He could go to the beach again!

HEAD TO HEAD

When Troy was growing up, his hero was Roger Staubach. Roger was one of Steve Young's heroes, too. Roger was the quarterback of the Dallas Cowboys from 1969–1979. Roger helped the Cowboys win two Super Bowls, the first two they ever won (Super Bowls VI in 1972 and XII in 1978). Dallas would not win another Super Bowl until Troy joined the team!

26 TROY AIKMAN

College rules state that when a player transfers schools, he can't play his first year at the new school. Because he had transferred, Troy could only practice with the team. He had to watch the games from the stands. But the next season, Troy was the starting quarterback for the UCLA Bruins.

Over the next two seasons, from 1987 to 1988, Troy became one of the best college quarterbacks ever. He completed 64.8 percent of his passes. He threw for 5,298 yards and 41 touchdowns. He had only 17 passes intercepted. Each season, UCLA's record was 10–2.

The only disappointment Troy felt at UCLA was not playing in the Rose Bowl. UCLA plays in the PAC-10 conference. Each year, the winner of the PAC-10 plays in the Rose Bowl against the winner of the Big 10. Many people think the Rose Bowl is the biggest bowl game of all. Every PAC-10 team has one goal: the Rose Bowl.

But both years, UCLA lost important games to the University of Southern California. USC and UCLA are both in Los Angeles. They are fierce rivals. The USC–UCLA game is always the biggest game of the season for the two schools.

In Troy's first year on the UCLA team, his team played USC on his 21st birthday. He should have stayed home and eaten cake and ice cream. He had his worst game of the season. While Troy had thrown only three interceptions all season, he threw three in this game alone! UCLA lost, 17–13. USC went to the Rose Bowl. The next season, Troy had a monster game. He completed a school-record 32 passes for 317 yards. He scored twice. Still, USC won again, this time by 31–22.

Even though they lost to USC, the UCLA Bruins played in other big bowl games. In 1987, UCLA beat Florida in the Aloha Bowl, 20–16. The next season, the Bruins defeated Arkansas in the Cotton Bowl, 17–3. Troy was an MVP in both bowl games.

Troy's college career was a huge success. He finished as UCLA's second all-time-leading passer. He was the third-highest-rated passer in NCAA college football history. Quarterback ratings measure passing yards, completions, attempts, touchdowns and interceptions.

He was a contender for that year's Heisman Trophy, which is awarded to the best player in college football. Even though he didn't win — he finished third, behind Barry Sanders (now with the Detroit Lions) and Rodney Peete (now with the Philadelphia Eagles) — Troy was still considered one of the outstanding prospects in football. Every pro team in the upcoming college draft would want him.

Troy's final college game, the Cotton Bowl, was played at Texas Stadium. It is the home of the Dallas Cowboys, Troy's favorite team. The Cowboys' coach, Tom Landry, watched Troy practice. Coach Landry and Troy sat next to each other at a dinner and talked. Troy met his hero,

Roger Staubach. The Cowboys wanted Troy to get used to the place. They hoped he'd be coming to play with them very soon.

So did the fans. Before the Cotton Bowl, Troy had become very popular in Dallas. The Cowboy fans wanted him to play there so much they started to experience "Aikmania!"

Why was everyone in Dallas so crazy about getting Troy? That season, the Cowboys had finished with a record of 3–13 — the worst record in the NFL. That meant they had the first pick in the college draft. They could choose any eligible college player they wanted.

The player they wanted was Troy Aikman.

4 EVEN COWBOYS GET THE BLUES

In April 1989, the Cowboys made Troy the first pick in the NFL Draft. The Dallas Cowboys got their man, and Troy Aikman got his team!

Things had changed for the Cowboys since Troy's visit to Dallas for the Cotton Bowl that past January. This was particularly true in the management of the team. This was because the Cowboys, who had been great and successful for many seasons, had fallen on hard times.

In the 1970's and early 1980's, Dallas was one of the best teams in the league. The Cowboys had played in four Super Bowls. They won twice. They had had some of the greatest players ever to play football. One of them was quarterback Roger Staubach, who had been Troy's idol when Troy was a kid.

The Cowboys also had the great Tom Landry as their coach. He had been the coach of the Cowboys since the team joined the NFL, in 1960. Coach Landry was a hero throughout Texas.

With all their success, the Cowboys had earned the

nickname "America's Team," because they had fans all over the country. (They also had people all around the country who didn't like them, but many were just jealous of the team's success.) The Dallas Cowboys were, perhaps, the most famous team in all of football, if not in all of sports.

But in the mid-1980's, the team struggled. After Roger retired in 1979, the Cowboys never found another great quarterback. Other star players also retired. (One of those was running back Calvin Hill, the father of today's NBA superstar Grant Hill.) Suddenly, the great Dallas Cowboys were not so great anymore. They had three-straight losing seasons. In 1988, they had a horrible 3–13 record — worst in the NFL!

In 1989, the Cowboys were put up for sale. Just two months before the draft, a man named Jerry Jones bought the team. He had made millions of dollars in the oil business. Mr. Jones immediately began to make changes. First, he fired Tom Landry, the only coach the Cowboys had ever had. The people of Dallas were shocked. They knew changes had to be made. Still, they couldn't imagine the Cowboys without Coach Landry.

Mr. Jones replaced Coach Landry with Jimmy Johnson. Mr. Jones and Coach Johnson were old friends. In fact, they had been teammates when they played football for the University of Arkansas.

The former teammates had only two months to prepare for the draft. With the worst record the year before, the Cowboys would pick first. Luckily, it didn't take much work to decide on the first pick. There was only one real choice: Troy Aikman. Coach Johnson finally would get his favorite quarterback! Everyone in the NFL agreed he was the best prospect that year — and one of the best quarterback prospects ever.

The Cowboys quickly showed how much they wanted Troy. They signed him to the richest rookie contract in NFL history! Troy's first contract was for six years. It called for a salary and benefits of $11 million.

Troy's happiness didn't last too long, however. In July, the NFL held a supplemental draft. That's when teams may draft players who weren't eligible or hadn't been picked in the first draft. In the supplemental draft, the Cowboys selected another good quarterback. His name was Steve Walsh. Steve had been the starting quarterback at the University of Miami, Jimmy Johnson's former team. Steve's teams had won 23 of 24 games while he was quarterback. In 1987, Miami won the national championship.

Troy wondered: Was Coach Johnson going to favor his old quarterback? He felt threatened. "I thought Jimmy had a natural allegiance [loyalty] to Steve," Troy told a newspaper reporter. "But the fact that he didn't make that clear or who he wanted for the future made the situation very tense."

The tension made Troy unhappy his rookie year. He

and Coach Johnson were not close. Even though Troy beat out Steve for the starting job, he never felt comfortable. He always wondered if Coach Johnson wanted to replace him. To make matters worse, the Cowboys didn't improve at all from their 3–13 record of the year before. In fact, they were even worse!

The Cowboys' offensive line was weak. Troy got pounded in every game because he wasn't being protected well. The team kept on losing. In the fourth game, Troy was hit so hard that he broke a finger on his left (non-throwing) hand. He missed the next five games.

Troy returned to the lineup in a game against the Phoenix Cardinals. This would be Troy's last chance to shine that season. He came through. He set a record for rookie quarterbacks by throwing for 379 yards! With less than two minutes to go, Troy threw for an 80-yard touch-

HEAD TO HEAD

Troy's first contract paid him an average of almost $2 million per year. The most money that his idol, Roger Staubah, ever made was $213,000. In 1945, another UCLA quarterback, named Bob Waterfield, took his pro team to an NFL Championship. His salary: $7,500. Talk about inflation!

down that put the Cowboys ahead. Unfortunately, Troy never saw the score. He was hit so hard on the play, he was knocked unconscious for eight minutes. Team doctors had to carry him off the field. Blood was flowing from his ear. In his book, Troy calls it one of the hardest hits he ever felt.

Troy stayed on the sidelines to see if his team could hold on to win. He was still groggy from the hit. The Cowboys couldn't stop the Cardinals. Phoenix won the game in the final seconds. The Cowboys finished the year with only one win and 15 losses. They were the worst team in the league for the second-straight year.

Dallas's only win came when Troy was injured and not playing. His record as a starting quarterback was 0–11. His other numbers were just as poor. He completed 155 of 293 passes (52.9 percent) for only 1,749 yards. He threw twice as many interceptions (18) as touchdowns (9). He had the worst rating of all starting quarterbacks in the NFL.

And Troy was hit so often, he felt like a punching bag. His whole body ached the entire season. (One newspaper story called him *"Ache*-man.") "I was so badly beaten up that I couldn't understand how some of my teammates had lasted 10 years in the NFL," Troy told *Sports Illustrated*. "I knew I'd never make it that long. There was nothing fun about football. It was time for a gut check."

The only good news about all this was that Troy's

rookie year was finally over. "That was probably as low as I got," Troy said a few years later. "I knew it couldn't get worse."

Things started to look up the next season. First, Steve Walsh was traded to New Orleans, in late September 1990. That made Troy the only offensive leader. His confidence grew each week. He also was learning more about the pro game. He could read defenses better and make better decisions. He began to work with his receivers better. His offensive line offered more protection.

Most important, Troy had a new teammate, a running back named Emmitt Smith. In the draft, the Cowboys picked Emmitt, the Heisman Trophy winner from Florida. With Dallas, Emmitt quickly developed into a runner who could break a game open. Now, other teams couldn't just concentrate on Troy and the Cowboys' passing game. They had to watch for Emmitt, too.

Even with these changes, the team didn't improve right away. It takes time for a team to come together. The Cowboys got off to another bad start. They lost seven of their first 10 games. (On the brighter side, the three wins were two more than they had had the whole season before!)

The constant losing began to get to Troy. He would complain to his agent, Leigh Steinberg. Troy would scream and yell about how awful it was, how much he hated losing, how he wanted to be traded to a winning team. The night before a game against the Los Angeles Rams, Troy exploded in anger. Mr. Steinberg listened quietly. Then he asked Troy where Troy really wanted to play.

"Dallas," Troy admitted. He knew he didn't really want a trade. Troy was just frustrated. He decided he would stick it out with the Cowboys. Troy knew that Jerry Jones and Jimmy Johnson were committed to making the Cowboys a winner. They wouldn't let all this losing continue forever.

The next day, Dallas beat the Rams, 24–21. Many people think that game was the beginning of the Cowboys' rise toward the Super Bowl.

After the Los Angeles victory, Dallas won three more games. Their four-straight victories made their record 7–7. It was the first time Dallas had been at .500 (meaning it had the same number of wins and losses) in many years. The Cowboys even had a chance to make the playoffs, which they hadn't made since 1985.

Just as things were looking brighter, disaster struck!

In the second-to-last game, against the Philadelphia Eagles, Troy was hurt again. In the first quarter, he was slammed to the ground. His shoulder was separated. He would be out for the season.

The Cowboys lost to the Eagles. They lost their last game, too, and missed the playoffs. Their final record was 7–9.

All in all, the team was happy. The Cowboys had

gone from being the worst team in the league to nearly making the playoffs.

Troy's numbers improved greatly, too. He completed 56.6 percent of his passes (226 of 399) for 2,579 yards. He still threw more interceptions than touchdowns. But the numbers were closer: 18 to 11.

Coach Johnson was pleased with the team's play. He gave a lot of the credit to Troy. "Even after losing the final two games, we came out of 1990 with a lot of positive feelings," Coach Johnson wrote in his book, *Turning Things Around*. "We'd won four games in a row and felt that without the injury to Troy, we'd have made the playoffs."

It was clear the Cowboys knew that Troy was the key.

5 MARCH TO THE SUPER BOWL

By now, everyone knew that the Cowboys depended on Troy. Even though they had other great players, like running back Emmitt Smith and wide receiver Michael Irvin, the Cowboys needed Troy and needed him to be happy.

Troy still had some concerns. He hadn't grown close to Coach Johnson. He also disagreed with Dallas's offensive coordinator, Dave Shula. Troy didn't like the offense Dave had designed. Coach Johnson knew he had to make a change. He replaced Dave with Norv Turner. Norv was Troy's kind of guy. Troy said Norv "was a guy I could relate to, be open with. He likes country music, he's down to Earth."

Troy also liked Norv's ideas about football. Norv liked an offense built around the passing game. He had liked the offense of the San Diego Chargers in the late 1970's and early 1980's. That offense was called "Air Coryell," after the Chargers' coach, Don Coryell. It featured a lot of passing.

Norv took that offense and molded it to fit Troy's way of playing. One of Troy's strengths as a quarterback is his quick release. He can see a receiver and throw the ball in an instant. Another strength is his ability to find open receivers. He has a knack for reading defenses. He can anticipate when and where a receiver will be open.

The Cowboys' new offense featured quick-release passes and ball control. Norv coached everyone to move faster. He taught the receivers to run different routes. They had to get open more quickly. They had to be at certain spots at exactly the right time to catch Troy's passes. (These are called timing routes or timing passes.) Even Troy had to become quicker. He had to speed up his footwork and his throwing motion.

All this coaching paid off. The Cowboys got off to their best start in many years. First, they beat the defending Super Bowl champion New York Giants. Troy was the star. The Cowboys were losing late in the game. They had the ball on their own 16-yard line. Troy directed their march toward the end zone. He completed four of five passes to get the Cowboys close. Then he threw one last pass. He hit Michael Irvin for the winning touchdown in the 21–16 victory! For the game, Troy completed an amazing 74 percent of his throws, for an impressive 277 total yards.

The next game, a win against Green Bay, he did even better. He completed 31 passes — the most in his career for one game. He finished the game by completing 12 passes in a row.

He followed that game by leading another last-second comeback. Troy averaged 12.6 yards per completion, his best ever, to lead Dallas to a big win over the Cincinnati Bengals.

The Cowboys were on a roll! They were 6–5 as they entered their 12th game. Troy was having his best year yet. That's why he was devastated when he got hurt again! In game 12, he injured his knee. For the second year in a row, he would miss the end of the season. He had now missed several games in each of his three seasons as a pro. People were starting to wonder why Troy, who was so big and strong, kept getting hurt. Was this a trend with him?

Coach Johnson wasn't worried, though. He told a reporter, "Troy's not injury prone. The position is injury prone." He knew that all quarterbacks get hurt. It's just a part of the job.

When Troy was hurt the previous year, the team lost its last two games. This season, the Cowboys did well without Troy. Troy's backup was now Steve Beuerlein. Steve led the Cowboys to victory in the team's last four games. The Cowboys finished with a record of 11–5. They made the playoffs for the first time in six seasons.

Troy could only watch from the sidelines. It was frustrating, but he rooted his teammates on. Steve helped Dallas beat the Chicago Bears, 17–13. In the second round,

Dallas faced the Detroit Lions. With the great Barry Sanders at running back, the Lions crushed the Cowboys. It was a rout: 38–6.

Even though Troy's season had ended early, he was happy with his improvement. His completion percentage (the percentage of the passes completed of the passes thrown) was up to 65.3 — a record for the Cowboys. He completed 237 of 363 passes for 2,754 yards. For the first time in his career, he threw more touchdown passes (11) than interceptions (10).

Troy's first year with Norv Turner as his offensive coordinator had been a huge success. Troy's completion percentage led the conference. So did his passing yardage. He was picked to play in the Pro Bowl — the NFL's all-star game — for the first time in his career.

All that sudden success excited everyone in Dallas. The fans were interested in seeing the Cowboys regain their championship form of the 1970's. Entering the 1992 season, the Cowboys' expectations were high. With Emmitt Smith and Michael Irvin, they had two of the great offensive players in the league. On defense, they had young stars like Ken Norton, Junior, and Russell Maryland. And in Troy, they had the league's best young quarterback. The only question: Could Troy stay healthy all year? He had never played a full season. If he could stay injury-free, the Cowboys had a chance to go all the way to the Super Bowl.

Troy answered his critics. He went the entire 1992–93 season without a serious injury. The Cowboys started the year by playing Washington. The Redskins were the defending Super Bowl champions. The game was televised on *Monday Night Football*, so the whole nation could see how the Cowboys had improved. Had they ever! They beat the Redskins, 23–10.

It was a great way to start the year. Wins kept rolling in. Troy led a late-game comeback against Denver. In a victory against Atlanta, Troy completed 85 percent of his passes.

The Cowboys won their division easily. Their record was 13–3. (Only three years earlier, it had been the exact opposite: 3–13!) In that short time, they had gone from last

HEAD TO HEAD

In the 1992 playoff for the National Football Conference title between Dallas and San Francisco, Troy passed for 322 yards. He completed an amazing 70 percent of his passes (24 of 34), an all-time playoff record! Steve Young wasn't too far behind. He completed 25 of 35 for 313 yards. He was sacked three times, score one touchdown, and was intercepted twice. The Cowboys beat the 49ers, 30–20.

place to champions of the NFC East.

During the regular season, Troy completed 302 of 473 passes (63.8 percent) for 3,445 yards. Troy had 23 touchdown passes and only 14 interceptions in 16 games. He threw almost twice as many touchdowns as interceptions. That was the opposite of his rookie year. Quite a turnaround!

He finished the regular season ranked third among all quarterbacks in the NFC. Could he match that level in the playoffs?

He did even better. He performed at record-breaking levels. The Cowboys' first playoff opponent was Philadelphia. The Eagles were no match for Dallas that day. The Cowboys destroyed Philadelphia, 34–10. Troy was outstanding. He threw 25 passes and completed 15, for 200 yards. He led the team on four long scoring drives. He called that victory "the biggest win I ever experienced." Even bigger wins were coming.

Next up: the San Francisco 49ers and their star quarterback, Steve Young.

The 49ers were favored to win that game. San Francisco had beat Dallas in six-straight games. But Troy would not let the Cowboys lose a seventh. Troy's most important throw of the day came late in the fourth quarter. The Cowboys were up by only 3 points. Steve Young was leading the 49ers on a comeback try. But Troy spotted

TROY AIKMAN 43

receiver Alvin Harper and threw him a perfect pass. The play went 70 yards! That pass set up a Cowboy touchdown. It clinched the win. Dallas had beat the 49ers, 30–20, and won the NFC. The Cowboys were going to the Super Bowl! Bring on the Buffalo Bills!

The Bills were the best team in the AFC for the third-straight year. They had appeared in the two previous Super Bowls. Unfortunately, their luck in the big game had not been good. In their first Super Bowl, they lost to the New York Giants. Their field goal kicker missed a last-second kick that would have won the game. At the end of the next season, they played the Washington Redskins. That time, the game wasn't close. The Bills lost in a blowout.

Still, they were an awesome team. Defensive end Bruce Smith was the league's best quarterback sacker. Quarterback Jim Kelly and running back Thurman Thomas led a high-scoring offense. Buffalo's no-huddle offense was nearly unstoppable. The team would run play after play without huddling. Buffalo played so quickly and ran so many plays without a rest, opposing team defenses couldn't catch their breath. The Bills just kept coming . . . and scoring.

Buffalo made it to its third-straight Super Bowl. No team had ever done that before. The Cowboys knew that the Bills would be desperate for a win. They would want to avenge their two-straight Super Bowl losses. But Dallas planned no mercy for Buffalo. Dallas won in a rout, 52–17. Thanks to Troy's statistics, good enough to make him MVP, Dallas was the NFL champion.

Troy's spectacular performance in the playoffs was the best in NFL history. He set several playoff records, including most yards per pass, lowest interception rate, and highest quarterback rating. Troy's post-season quarterback rating was an unbelievable 116.7 — the highest ever in post-season play. In addition, Troy had eight touchdown passes in three playoff games.

It had been quite a season. Troy started the season just hoping to stay healthy and have a winning percentage. Now, Troy was a Super Bowl hero! He was one of the most famous athletes in America.

6

REPEAT!

Troy Aikman was now a superstar. After the Super Bowl, he appeared on all the TV talk shows. He was asked to appear at many functions, such as award ceremonies and dinners. He was swamped with offers to endorse products. He was recognized as one of the two or three best quarterbacks in the league.

Troy refused to get a big head about it. After he won the Super Bowl MVP, he promised not to change. "So many players, once they get into a situation like this, take it too far," he said. "They lose focus as to what actually got them to that position. I won't do anything that's going to take away from preparing for the upcoming season. I'm not playing football for the endorsements."

He also knew that his fame was based on the team's success, not his. "No one was calling me when we were 1–15," he joked.

Troy was at the top of his game. But he was near the bottom when it came to salary. Twenty-four starting quarterbacks made more money. There were even some *backup* quarterbacks who were paid more than Troy. He was unhappy about that. People thought he should hold out — refuse to play until the Cowboys signed him to a new contract. But he wouldn't do that. That wasn't how Troy acted.

"I will not sit out of camp forcing anybody to renegotiate my contract," he said. "I've always felt that if you sign a contract, then you fulfill it."

That was an honorable decision. Many players would have sulked and pouted. Many would not have played. Troy honored his commitment. He played as hard as ever. (The Cowboys appreciated his actions. By the end of the season, they signed Troy to a new contract.)

In addition to his contract, Troy had other worries at the beginning of the 1993 season. He was coming off back surgery. While lifting weights in May, during the off-season, Troy felt something pop in his back.

At first he was too busy to have it checked out. Then he went to quarterback training camp and practiced for two days. He could tell his back wasn't right. He wanted to have it examined, but doctors told him they thought the problem wasn't serious. They felt it had something to do with his muscles and that his back would get better with time. But it didn't heal, so Troy had an MRI, an imaging method somewhat like an X-ray.

The MRI revealed damage in one of the disks that made up Troy's spinal column. A damaged disk can be a serious problem. If it's not treated, it can lead to permanent problems, such as paralysis. Troy was very concerned. It was decided that Troy needed surgery to repair the bulging disk. He had an operation at the end of June and it was successful. After some tough rehabilitation to get his strength back, Troy was finally ready to start working with his teammates in September. He even came back a few weeks early!

Although Troy was back, his best runner was not. Emmitt Smith, like Troy, wanted a new contract. Unlike Troy, Emmitt decided to hold out and not play until he got one. With Emmitt out, the Cowboys lost their first two games of the season. One of the losses was to the Buffalo Bills, the same team they had crushed just a few months earlier in the Super Bowl.

This was a serious blow to the Cowboy's chances at another Super Bowl. No team had ever won a Super Bowl after starting the season 0–2.

But Troy wouldn't let that fact stop him. In the next 12 games, he led his team to 10 wins. (Troy had some help from Emmitt, too. Emmitt returned to the lineup after the team lost those first two games.) When the team's record was 10–4, the Cowboys' owner, Jerry Jones, knew he needed to pay Troy what Troy deserved. Remember, Troy had been playing without a new contract. Mr. Jones then signed Troy to a contract that would last for eight years. He would most likely be a Cowboy for the rest of his career. For that kind of commitment, Dallas would pay him $50 million. It made Troy the highest paid player in NFL history.

Troy was happy to stay with Dallas, because the Cowboys had committed to making the team a winner. The organization "will do what has to be done to be competitive," Troy said when he announced his new contract.

With the pressure of signing a new contract over, Troy got back to business. He and the Cowboys won their final two games of the regular season. They finished with a 12–4 record and won the NFC East again. They also won the home-field advantage for the playoffs. They would have the friendly fans at Texas Stadium cheering them on. Winning one Super Bowl is hard enough. Winning two in a row had been done only four times.

The Cowboys marched past Green Bay in the conference semi-finals. Troy threw three touchdown passes, and Dallas beat the Packers, 27–17. That set up another confer-

HEAD TO HEAD

In the 1993 NFC conference playoff game between Dallas and San Francisco, here's how Troy stacked up against Steve: Troy completed 14 of 18 passes for 177 yards and two touchdowns. Steve completed 27 of 45 for 287 yards. He scored one touchdown, was intercepted once, and was sacked four times. The Cowboys came out on top, 38–21.

ence final against San Francisco. This one wasn't as close, though. The Cowboys won, 38–21 *(see box)*.

Ask him about the game against the 49ers, though, and Troy will draw a blank. Early in the third quarter, he was smacked in the head — hard. Troy was kneed in the helmet by a lineman. The hit caused a concussion. He left the game and watched from the sidelines. After the game, he couldn't remember anything.

Troy was groggy the rest of the day. Doctors thought he should spend the night in a hospital. He was so fuzzy-headed that when someone asked him who the MVP of the last Super Bowl was, he couldn't remember — even though it was Troy! When doctors asked Troy where the next Super Bowl was being played, he answered, "Henryetta?"

Wrong, Troy. It wasn't being played in your hometown. It was to be played in Atlanta, Georgia. He and his teammates were going to the Super Bowl again.

And who would they play? Buffalo again! The Bills had made it to their fourth-straight Super Bowl, a truly amazing feat. Many fans were growing tired of Buffalo. Every year the Bills played in the Super Bowl. And every year they lost — each time by a bigger and bigger margin. The Bills players didn't care about that, though. Their team motto was WE'RE BACK. DEAL WITH IT!

Dallas dealt with it just fine. The Cowboys destroyed the Bills once again. This time the score was 30–13. Dallas had repeated as Super Bowl champions!

In spite of the lopsided score, Troy was still not at his best in this game. The concussion still affected him. He admitted in his book, *Things Change,* "The first two quarters it looked as though maybe I should have taken the day off. My timing was rusty and we were frustrated."

The Cowboys were actually behind at halftime, 13–6. But in the third quarter, James Washington returned a Buffalo fumble for a touchdown. The Cowboys cruised the rest of the way. Emmitt Smith was the star of the game. Emmitt scored two touchdowns, and he ran for 132 yards total. For his super efforts, Emmitt was voted Most Valuable Player of the game. The Dallas defense had been spectacular, too. They shut out the Bills in the second half while the Dallas offense scored 24 points to take control.

And despite his concussion, Troy did his part. He was 19 of 27, for 207 yards. He was intercepted once. He joined an elite group of players. Only four NFL quarterbacks had won back-to-back Super Bowls. Bart Starr did it with Green Bay in 1966 and '67. Bob Griese did it with Miami in 1972 and '73. Terry Bradshaw did it *twice* with Pittsburgh in 1974 and '75, and 1978 and '79. Joe Montana did it with San Francisco in 1988 and '89. The first three are in the Hall Of Fame. Joe is sure to be there soon. And now, Troy was in their company.

For the season, Troy had remarkable stats. He threw only six interceptions all season. He completed 271 of 392 passes (69.1 percent), for 3,100 yards and 15 touchdowns.

His quarterback rating of 99.0 was second-best in Cowboy history. Only Roger Staubach's 104.8 rating, in 1971, had been higher. Now Troy had two Super Bowl rings, just as Roger did. Roger finally had some competition in Dallas. Cowboy fans once thought that no one could ever replace Roger. Now, Troy was making them forget their favorite (and his!) all-time quarterback. The two had become equals in the hearts and minds of Cowboy fans everywhere.

Even Roger was ready to share the spotlight. He called Troy the best quarterback in the NFL. Not everyone gets that kind of tribute from their boyhood idol!

7 ONCE AND FUTURE CHAMPS

In pro football, things change quickly. Players change teams frequently. Free agency means that players can pick the team they want to play for. Coaches move, too. When a team is successful, other teams want their players and coaches. That's what happened to the Cowboys.

In 1994, the Cowboys changed. Several key players left. Linebacker Ken Norton, Jr., went to San Francisco as a free agent. Two other defensive starters, Tony Casillas and Thomas Everett, also left. The Cowboys lost offensive lineman Kevin Gogan.

One of the biggest losses to Troy was the departure of offensive coordinator Norv Turner. Norv had helped make Troy a star. Now Norv was going to be a head coach of the Washington Redskins.

The biggest change was that of the Cowboys' own head coach. Jimmy Johnson had been clashing with owner Jerry Jones. Even though they had been friends since college, they often fought. Mr. Jones thought Coach Johnson was trying to be the boss. Coach Johnson thought Mr. Jones was interfering with his coaching. Finally, the two agreed they could not work together. After taking a 1–15 team to two-straight Super Bowl victories, Jimmy Johnson left the Cowboys.

Dallas fans couldn't believe it. How could such a successful team break up? They were just reaching their peak. Writers and football fans were calling Dallas a dynasty. They meant they were expected to remain champions for a long, long time. Now, fans had doubts. Could the Cowboys recover from all these changes and still defend their title?

Troy was especially hurt. Not only was he still close to Norv Turner, he had finally grown close to Coach Johnson. Their relationship had started slowly. Over the years, though, they found common interests. Coach Johnson loves tropical fish tanks. He helped Troy set one up in Troy's house. The two of them often talked about fish. They learned to love sitting around, talking about football and fish and other favorite things. Troy was going to miss his coach.

He wasn't thrilled with Coach Johnson's replacement, either. It was his first college coach, Barry Switzer. Troy still had some bad feelings about his treatment at Oklahoma.

Coach Switzer hadn't coached in a long time. He had left the University of Oklahoma in 1989. His team had been troubled by scandals. The Sooners were placed on probation by the NCAA. Barry had resigned under a cloud of scandal having to do with illegal payments to players and other rules violations.

Coach Switzer had never coached in the pros. People wondered how he would handle the job. There was also the pressure to win a third-straight Super Bowl. No team had ever done that.

In spite of all this difficulty, the Cowboys performed well. They finished 12–4, behind 13–3 San Francisco in the NFC.

In the divisional playoff, Troy was flawless. The Cowboys beat Green Bay, 35–9. Troy completed 25 passes for 337 yards and two TDs. One of the touchdowns was a 94-yarder to Alvin Harper. It was the longest touchdown pass play in playoff history. Troy did all this despite the fact that he was playing with a sprained knee. He played the entire game in a leg brace.

For the third-straight year, the Cowboys played Steve Young and the 49ers in the NFC Championship. A victory would send the Cowboys to their third-straight Super Bowl.

This time, though, the 49ers had the best record in the NFL. They had beaten Dallas in the regular season and had home-field advantage for the NFC Championship game.

Many Dallas players were injured. The Cowboys turned the ball over three times in the first eight minutes. One turnover came when Troy's third pass was picked off and returned for a touchdown. San Francisco took advan-

TROY AIKMAN 55

tage of Dallas's sloppy play. It grabbed a 21–0 lead in the first quarter behind Steve Young.

Troy tried to rally his teammates. He wrote about it in his book: "'Hey, we're fine,' I told teammates on the sideline. 'We're going to win this thing. We're not out of it.'"

The team fought hard. With just under two minutes left, they still had a chance. But they found themselves with fourth down and 18 yards to go on the San Francisco 46. Troy's last pass fell short. Dallas couldn't catch up. The Cowboys lost, 38–28. For Dallas, there would be no "three-peat."

After the game, Troy shook hands with Steve. "I'm happy for you," Troy told him. "Good luck against San Diego." Steve didn't need any luck, though. The 49ers crushed the Chargers in Super Bowl XXIX.

Troy felt disappointed, of course. "Losing such a big game is painful and leaves an empty feeling," he wrote. "It

HEAD TO HEAD

Troy's house in Dallas is right next to one where former Pittsburgh Steeler quarterback Terry Bradshaw lived. When Terry was with Pittsburgh, he won four Super Bowls. Together with Troy's three, that's seven Super Bowl rings between these next door neighbors. Quite a neighborhood!

hurts worse when a team makes mistakes, as we did." Still, he was proud of his teammates. They had tried as hard as they could and almost pulled off a tremendous feat.

Besides, they had next season to look forward to.

The entire team was excited. All the players were looking to regain their glory in 1995–96. Missing the Super Bowl made everyone hungry to return to the championship. Troy and his teammates all reported to training camp in the best shape of their lives. Even though the team had lost Pro Bowl center Mark Stepnoski and wide receiver Alvin Harper to free agency, they were determined to avenge the previous season's disappointment.

They got right to work. In the first game of the season, Dallas shut out the New York Giants, 35–0. Emmitt Smith ran for a 60-yard touchdown on his first carry of the season! The Cowboys were on their way! They cruised through the regular season. They won their division again, with a 12–4 record.

Every year, before the playoffs, Troy meets with Roger Staubach. They have dinner together. Roger says what he thinks of the Cowboys, what kind of season they had, and how they can do well in the playoffs. Troy listens closely to his former idol, now his peer. Roger's experience of playing in four Super Bowls means a lot to Troy. And Roger likes helping Troy prepare for the post-season. "I enjoy being someone [Troy] is able to talk to about similar circumstances," Roger told reporter Kevin Lyons of *The Fort Worth Star-Telegram.*

Whatever Roger told Troy at the 1996 dinner meeting must have worked: the Cowboys rolled through the playoffs.

Their first opponent was Philadelphia. The Eagles had beaten Dallas, 20–17, only one month earlier. Dallas came into this game hurt. Troy's legs were sore. Defensive end Charles Haley was out for the season, recovering from back surgery. But the Cowboys overcame these problems to stop the Eagles easily, 30–11. Troy was 17 for 24, for 253 yards and one touchdown. Next up: The Green Bay Packers.

Texas Stadium was packed with 65,135 ecstatic fans. A win would send the 'Boys back to the Super Bowl. But the Packers were a tough team. They were led by quarterback Brett Favre. Brett had been the MVP of the regular season. Troy wanted to win this game very badly.

The game was tight and pressure-packed. Dallas took an early 11-point advantage, 14–3. But Green Bay fought back to take a 17–14 lead behind Brett Favre's two long touchdown passes. Soon after, Chris Boniol kicked a field goal for the Cowboys to tie it at 17–17.

When the Cowboys got the ball back, Troy and Emmitt put on a show. Dallas was stuck on its own one-yard line. The two of them marched off on a 99-yard touchdown drive! Eleven plays later, Emmitt scored to put Dallas on top, 24–17. That was the score at halftime.

But the Pack came back again. They regained the lead by scoring 10 points on their first two possessions in the second half. The score was 27–24 for Green Bay after three quarters.

The fourth quarter belonged to Dallas. They scored two touchdowns, sacked Brett three times, and had a key interception to stop a Packer drive. After this interception, Emmitt scored his third touchdown of the day. The win was sealed, 38–27.

After the game, Troy presented Coach Switzer with the game ball. That's an award usually given to the Most Valuable Player of the game. Troy and his coach had had some disagreements during the regular season. Troy gave Coach Switzer the game ball to let him know he appreciated his efforts. But Troy didn't want to make too big of a deal of his gesture. He knew there was more work ahead.

"There is still something left for this football team to achieve," Troy said after the game. "I know that I'm not content, and I don't think the team is."

They wanted to win the Super Bowl.

Sun Devil Stadium, in Tempe, Arizona, was the site of Super Bowl XXX. The Cowboys were favored to beat their opponents, the Pittsburgh Steelers. In fact, many experts predicted another Super Bowl blowout. But the experts were wrong. It was the best Super Bowl since the

Giants had edged Buffalo by 1 point five years earlier.

It didn't start out as a good game, however. The Cowboys scored a touchdown and two field goals on their first three possessions! Just before halftime, they led, 13–0. It looked like another rout. But as the half was ending, Pittsburgh mounted a 13-play, 54-yard drive. Quarterback Neil O'Donnell threw a six-yard touchdown pass to receiver Yancey Thigpen only 13 seconds before the half. It was a close game again: Dallas 13, Pittsburgh 7.

Dallas scored first in the second half to go up, 20–7. But Troy and the offensive unit didn't have much chance to add to the lead. Pittsburgh held the ball for more than 21 minutes of the 30-minute half. The Dallas defense played superbly. The defense blitzed and rattled Neil into making many bad throws. But because they were on the field so long, they were tired.

With 11:20 left in the game, Pittsburgh's Norm Johnson kicked a 46-yard field goal to cut Dallas' lead to 20–10. Then the Steelers fooled the Cowboys. They tried an on-side kick! The Cowboys weren't expecting it, and Pittsburgh recovered the ball. The weary Dallas defense had to return to the field without a rest. They had been on the field for 20 straight plays when Pittsburgh running back Bam Morris scored. The score was now 20–17 with 6:36 left to play.

The Cowboys got the next kickoff, but could not move the football. They had to punt. Pittsburgh had a chance to take the lead. They started what could have been a game-winning drive toward Dallas's end zone. But on the second play of the drive, quarterback Neil O'Donnell threw a terrible pass. There was no receiver in sight. The pass was picked off by cornerback Larry Brown — Larry's second interception of the game. There was only 4:09 left. Could the Cowboys hold on to the ball and run out the clock?

Yes! This time, Dallas's offense produced. Emmitt Smith scored from four yards out. That clinched the victory. Dallas had won its third Super Bowl in four years! The dynasty was back!

Troy was 15 of 23 for 209 yards, one touchdown and no interceptions. He became the first quarterback to win three championships before the age of 30. Not even Roger had done that!

In fact, no one has done what Troy has accomplished. Not Roger. Not Terry Bradshaw. Not Joe Montana. Troy has won 10 of his last 11 playoff games. He holds career playoff records for completion percentage and average gain per pass. He also holds the record for the longest single pass play (94 yards) in playoff history.

And he has those three Super Bowl rings. With all these accomplishments, Troy has to be considered the quarterback of the 1990's. The Pro Football Hall of Fame can reserve a spot for Troy Aikman.

Not bad for a kid who really wanted to play baseball!

8

A SHY SUPERSTAR

A newspaper writer once wrote the following about Troy. "Friends say [Troy is] pretty much what he appears to be. He's soft-spoken and shy, a private man in a public position."

It would be easy for Troy to have a big ego. "Hollywood could have created him," said CBS Sports' reporter Lesley Visser in *People* magazine. "A blond, blue-eyed cowboy with perfect teeth and a hot hand. Troy looks exactly like the hero he's become."

His agent calls him "a marketing dream." Troy can endorse as many products as he wants.

His teammates love him. "I attribute my success to him," Michael Irvin told *Sports Illustrated*. "The greatest things, the greatest times — Troy is 100 percent responsible, and even then I'm understating it."

Even with all this praise, Troy refuses to become a big shot. Of course, he has signed up to endorse a few products, but he won't go overboard. You won't see his face on every billboard and in every commercial. That's just not his way. He plans to stay humble and low-key.

He even makes jokes about his fame. When *People* magazine voted him one of its 50 most beautiful people, he joked, "Well, they must not know very many people."

Troy prefers the home lights to the limelight. He likes to relax at his house near Dallas. He loves to listen to country music. He "surfs the net" on his home computer. He even takes a laptop with him on the road. He studies game plans (and probably plays computer games!). Troy likes computers so much he once asked his agent, "Do you think I'm turning into a computer nerd?"

Mostly he enjoys hanging out with friends and family.

He does like some parts of being famous. He got to appear on the TV show *Coach*. He played himself. (After all, he's a football player, not an actor!) He's friendly with the members of the country group Shenandoah. He appeared in their music video. He also appeared on stage at Farm Aid, a concert that raised money for needy farmers and their families.

Troy likes to communicate with other famous athletes. Before the 1994 winter Olympics, he sent figure skater Nancy Kerrigan a telegram wishing her luck. He also sent a telegram of congratulation to Baltimore Oriole shortstop Cal Ripken, Junior, when Cal broke Lou Gehrig's record for consecutive games played, on September 6, 1995.

Troy does a lot of work for charity. In 1991, he started the Troy Aikman Foundation. His group gives money to children's charities in the Dallas-Fort Worth area. He actively supports lots of charities in his hometown, too. In 1991, he helped raise $225,000 to build a health-and-fitness center for kids in Henryetta. He also sponsors a college scholarship for financially needy students from his old high school.

Troy is so involved with these and other good causes that he has been a finalist for the NFL Man of the Year award several times. That award goes to NFL players who contribute to their community.

But Troy's biggest love is still football. With all his success, and in spite of his injuries, Troy expects to keep playing for a long time. "I've heard athletes who've retired come out and say, 'Well, there was nothing left to prove. I've done it all, and that's why I'm getting out.'" he said in *Sports Illustrated*. "I don't buy that."

He's already won three Super Bowls, but that's no reason to stop. "There's always another one to win," Troy says, "in whatever it is you do."

TROY AIKMAN'S CAREER PASSING STATS

COLLEGE STATS
University of Oklahoma

Seasons	Games	Attempts	Completions	Pct.	Yards	TD's	*Int.
1984	3	20	6	30.0	41	0	3
1985	4	47	27	57.4	442	1	1

UCLA

1987	12	273	178	65.2	2527	17	8
1988	12	354	228	64.4	2771	24	9
TOTALS	31	694	439	54.2	5,781	42	21

PRO STATS
Dallas Cowboys

Seasons	Games	Attempts	Completions	Pct.	Yards	TD's	*Int.
1989	11	293	155	52.9	1,749	9	18
1990	15	399	226	56.6	2,579	11	18
1991	12	363	237	65.3	2,754	11	10
1992	16	473	302	63.8	3,445	23	14
1993	14	392	271	69.1	3,100	15	6
1994	14	361	233	64.5	2,678	13	12
1995	16	432	280	64.8	3,304	16	7
TOTALS	98	2,713	1,704	62.4	19,609	98	85

* Int. — Interceptions

When Troy joined the Cowboys in 1989, they weren't a good team. Four seasons later, he and the 'Boys won the Super Bowl. By 1996, they had won three!

When Troy was a kid, he dreamed of being a pro baseball player. In his senior year in high school, he even got a call from a major league scout!

Courtesy of the Aikman family

The Aikman family in late '95 *(clockwise from upper left)*: **dad Ken, mom Charlyn, sister Terri, her fiancé Dave, brother-in-law Mike, nephew Drew, and sister Tammy.**

Peter Read Miller/Sports Illustrated

After starting his college career at Oklahoma, Troy transferred to UCLA *(above)*. UCLA made good use of Troy's ability to throw accurate passes.

Running back Emmitt Smith *(center)* and receiver Michael Irvin *(right)* teamed up with Troy to bring Dallas to the Super Bowl again and again.

When Troy helped Dallas beat Pittsburgh in the Super Bowl in 1996, he became the first quarterback to win three NFL championships before the age of 30!

THERE ARE MANY WAYS IN WHICH **STEVE'S** AND **TROY'S** LIVES HAVE BEEN ALIKE...

BOTH BOYS' FAMILIES MOVED. **STEVE** MOVED AT AGE 8 FROM A SUBURB IN UTAH TO A SUBURB OF NEW YORK CITY. **TROY** LIVED IN A CALIFORNIA SUBURB, AND THEN AT AGE 12 MOVED TO A RANCH IN OKLAHOMA...

DAD — I DON'T THINK I'LL EVER LIKE LIVING HERE...

SURE YOU WILL, SON!

BOTH EXCELLED AT SEVERAL SPORTS IN HIGH SCHOOL AND WON FOOTBALL SCHOLARSHIPS TO COLLEGE. BOTH STRUGGLED AS FRESHMEN ALTHOUGH **TROY** STARTED ONE GAME THAT YEAR AT THE **UNIVERSITY OF OKLAHOMA**. AT **BRIGHAM YOUNG UNIVERSITY**, **STEVE** HAD **SEVEN** QUARTERBACKS AHEAD OF HIM!

NEXT SEASON, WE MIGHT HAVE YOU TRY A DIFFERENT POSITION!

BY JUNIOR YEAR, *STEVE* WAS THE STAR OF THE *BYU* TEAM. HIS SENIOR YEAR, THE TEAM WAS 11-1! MEANWHILE *TROY* TRANSFERRED TO *UCLA*. WITH HIM AT QUARTERBACK, THE *BRUINS* WERE 20-4.

"THIS GUY CAME OUT OF NOWHERE AND HE BROKE 13 OFFENSIVE RECORDS!"

"THANK GOODNESS *TROY* WANTED TO COME BACK TO CALIFORNIA — HE'S GREAT!"

THEN THE TWO TOOK DIFFERENT PATHS. IN 1984, INSTEAD OF JOINING THE *NFL*, *STEVE* SIGNED WITH THE *U.S. FOOTBALL LEAGUE*. HE WAS GIVEN A BIG CONTRACT.

BYU'S STEVE YOUNG HAS SIGNED ON WITH THE TWO-YEAR-OLD U.S.F.L.'S L.A. EXPRESS FOR A STAGGERING $40 MILLION!

TROY WAS SELECTED FIRST IN THE 1989 *NFL* DRAFT BY THE *DALLAS COWBOYS*. HE HAD A TERRIBLE ROOKIE SEASON...

I WONDER IF THIS KID IS ANY GOOD? THE TEAM HAS ONLY WON ONE GAME AND LOST SIXTEEN!

TROY AND THE COWBOYS IMPROVED STEADILY. IN JANUARY 1993, HE LED THE TEAM TO THE SUPER BOWL. HE DID SO WELL THERE, HE WAS CHOSEN MVP!

I CAN'T BELIEVE THE COWBOYS ARE WINNING THE SUPER BOWL BY A SCORE OF 52-17!

STEVE DECIDED TO JOIN THE NFL. IN 1987, HE JOINED THE SAN FRANCISCO 49ERS, WHERE HE WAS MADE THE BACKUP TO JOE MONTANA. IN 1991, STEVE BECAME THE STARTING QUARTERBACK. HE WON THE SUPER BOWL IN JANUARY 1995, AND HE, TOO, WAS NAMED SUPER BOWL MVP!

Steve won two MVP titles in three years with the
49ers, but didn't win the fans over until
he and the team won the Super Bowl, in 1995.

Baseball was only one of the sports
Steve played at Eastern Junior High School.
He also played football and basketball.

Following in his father's footsteps, Steve attended Brigham Young University. It took until his junior year before he played regularly.

Peter Read Miller/Sports Illustrated

Instead of joining the NFL, Steve signed with
the USFL's L.A. Express. But the league didn't last long,
partly because it didn't have many fans!

It was not easy for Steve when he joined
the 49ers in 1987. San Francisco already had
a star quarterback in Joe Montana. For four years,
Steve didn't get to play very often.

John W. McDonough/Sports Illustrated

Tom DiPace

Because Troy's team and Steve's team are in the same conference, only one of them can go to the Super Bowl. In 1993, '94, and '96, it was Troy. In 1995, Steve took a turn and beat San Diego, 49–26.

STEVE YOUNG'S CAREER PASSING STATS

COLLEGE
Brigham Young University

Season	Games	Attempts	Completions	Pct.	Yards	TD's	*Int.
1981	10	112	56	50.0	731	5	5
1982	11	367	230	62.7	3,100	18	18
1983	11	429	306	71.3	3,902	33	10
Totals	32	908	592	65.2	7,733	56	33

PRO
USFL Los Angeles Express

Season	Games	Attempts	Completions	Pct.	Yards	TD's	*Int.
1984	12	310	179	57.7	2,361	10	9
1985	13	250	137	54.8	1,741	6	13
Totals	25	560	316	56.4	4,102	16	22

NFL Tampa Bay Buccaneers

Season	Games	Attempts	Completions	Pct.	Yards	TD's	*Int.
1985	5	138	72	52.2	935	3	8
1986	14	363	195	53.7	2,282	8	13

NFL San Francisco 49ers

Season	Games	Attempts	Completions	Pct.	Yards	TD's	*Int.
1987	8	69	37	53.6	570	10	0
1988	11	101	54	53.5	680	3	3
1989	10	92	64	69.6	1,001	8	3
1990	6	62	38	61.3	427	2	0
1991	11	279	180	64.5	2,517	17	8
1992	16	402	268	66.7	3,465	25	7
1993	16	462	314	68.0	4,023	29	16
1994	16	461	324	70.3	3,969	35	10
1995	11	447	299	66.9	3,200	20	11
Totals	124	2,876	1,845	64.2	23,069	160	79

* Int. — Interceptions

feel as much pressure going into the 1995 season. He didn't have anything left to prove. Maybe he could just relax and enjoy playing the game.

On October 11, 1995, Steve turned 34. Four days later, during a game against Indianapolis, he injured his throwing shoulder. Steve missed the next five games. Green Bay knocked the 49ers out of the playoffs. There would be no San Francisco-Dallas rematch in the NFC Championship Game. Troy and Dallas did make it to the Super Bowl, and beat the Pittsburgh Steelers, 27–17.

Steve wants to win more championships. "The essence of Steve Young always has been an incredible desire to win and be the best at everything," Steve's agent, Leigh Steinberg, says.

Steve is, along with Troy, among the best quarterbacks playing in the NFL today. He is an exceptionally accurate passer and an outstanding runner. Other teams never know what he will do — run or throw? It's hard to defend against a guy like that, who can do both so well.

San Francisco fans complained for years that Steve Young was not Joe Montana, and they were right. Steve, in many ways, was better. At BYU, and at San Francisco, Steve was compared to the starting quarterbacks who came before him. In 13 years in the pros, Steve has emerged as a star in his own right, one that quarterbacks of the future will be measured against for many years to come.

held it close. There were tears in Steve's eyes as he held the trophy.

Someone in the crowd of reporters yelled, "Speech!"

"If you keep playing, sooner or later they'll hand you a trophy and then you hug it as hard as you can!" Steve said.

After the Super Bowl, the 49ers took a trip to Disney World in Orlando, Florida. Steve and Jerry stood on a parade float with Mickey Mouse. Steve stood on one side of Mickey and Jerry stood on the other. Steve had to laugh as he heard two boys talking. Although Steve and Jerry thought they were famous, the children had no idea who they were. Steve heard one boy say to the other, "You can't get near [Mickey], those two big guys won't let you." For all the two boys knew, Mickey had two big bodyguards!

That June, Steve flew home to Greenwich. He visited Greenwich High School and gave his old math teacher, Terry Lowe, the 1994 NFL Teacher of the Year award. (Steve had nominated Mr. Lowe, and Mr. Lowe had won!) Then Steve spoke to the students.

"Don't think anything special happened to me," Steve said to the students with his usual modesty. "All I did was keep going . . . I just kept walking, step after step. Every time someone said I couldn't do something, I kept walking — I wasn't sure I could do it — but I kept going forward."

Now that he had won the Super Bowl, Steve didn't

points seemed the right way to celebrate.

As part of the celebration, the Niners dumped Gatorade all over Coach Seifert. He just smiled. Up in the stands, a San Francisco fan held up his right hand and pointed to his five fingers. He was pointing out the fact that San Francisco had just won its fifth Super Bowl. No team had ever won five Super Bowls! Not even Dallas!

Steve looked over the crowd and held up his helmet to his family, his friends, and the San Francisco fans. Winning the Super Bowl was one of the happiest events in Steve's life. He had been the starting quarterback and this was a moment he had been dreaming of all his life.

"The Super Bowl was the only thing that was better than the dream itself," Steve said after the game.

Steve, who had been named the NFL Most Valuable Player at the end of the 1994 regular season, was now named Super Bowl MVP! After the game, Steve grabbed the winner's Vince Lombardi Trophy in the locker room and

HEAD TO HEAD

Steve was with the 49ers for three Super Bowl victories, but the important one to him was the one he won in 1995 as the starting quarterback. Troy has won three Super Bowls with the Cowboys.

many as 19 points. They were close.

Steve ran out the field for the start of the game with his right fist held high. He didn't waste time helping San Francisco score once the game began. Less than a minute and a half into it, Steve threw the ball deep to Jerry Rice. Jerry saw the ball spiraling toward him. He cut away from two safeties and grabbed it. The 49er fans whooped and cheered watching Jerry run 44 yards for a touchdown. No team had ever scored that quickly in a Super Bowl!

Before the first quarter ended, Steve threw another touchdown pass deep down the middle of the field. This time, it was a 51-yard pass to Ricky Watters. Ricky reached up to grab the ball, broke away from two San Diego tacklers, and dashed for the end zone. The 49ers led, 14–0!

By halftime, Steve had done something extraordinary — he had thrown four touchdown passes. In his best *games* ever, he had thrown four touchdown passes. Here he was in the Super Bowl, and he had thrown four TD's before the game was half over. The 49ers had a 28–10 lead.

At 3:18 in the third quarter, Jerry caught yet another pass from Steve for a fifth touchdown. In the fourth quarter, Steve again threw to Jerry, who tumbled into the end zone for *another* touchdown. No quarterback had ever thrown *six* touchdowns at a Super Bowl!

The 49ers beat the Chargers, 49–26. If you add up all the points, you'll come up with a total of 75. It was the NFL's 75th anniversary in 1995. Seventy-five Super Bowl

8

A DREAM COME TRUE

For the 1994 season, the San Francisco players had but one goal, according to center Bart Oates: to beat Dallas in the NFC championship game.

On January 15, 1995, San Francisco did! Steve completed nearly half his passes. He threw two touchdowns and ran for another one. The 49ers beat Dallas for the first time in three years! Rick Telander of *Sports Illustrated* wrote that Steve ran around Candlestick Park holding the game ball "like a kid showing off his first A paper."

Steve could not hold back his joy at finally winning this important game. Now it was on to Miami for the Super Bowl. In Florida, Steve would have the chance to prove that he could win the world championship!

The 49ers faced the San Diego Chargers at Super Bowl XXIX. The Chargers were the American Football Conference champions. The Super Bowl was set for January 29, 1995.

People predicted that this Super Bowl would be a blowout. They predicted that San Francisco would win by as pulled Steve out of the game, concerned for his safety.

"He took that last hit and I said, 'The [heck] with this. I'm taking him out,'" the coach told Ray Ratto of the *San Francisco Examiner.*

Steve threw a fit when his backup, Elvis Grbac, tapped him on the shoulder to take over. Steve wanted to finish the game, no matter how bad it was. He screamed at Coach Seifert and pushed away players who tried to calm him down. He paced the sideline until the end of the game.

This defeat, and Steve's outburst, had an unexpected effect. The 49ers respected Steve for getting angry and showing how he really felt.

"What it did was, it made him realize he's going to stand up and start being a leader, and he's going to start saying what he thinks, instead of just keeping it to himself," said San Francisco tight end Brent Jones. "I think this team is looking for that kind of . . . leadership. He definitely has earned the respect of the guys by his toughness. . . ."

"He's finally seeing that this is his team," said Niner safety Tim McDonald.

Steve was surprised that it had a positive result. "If I'd known better, I'd have yelled at my dad when I was ten years old," Steve said kiddingly to the press.

The media said that when Steve got angry at his coach, it was a turning point in his career. Steve put on quite a show during the rest of that season!

lives throwing touchdowns or interceptions," Steve said.

Steve wasn't about to give up playing football, however. He began his eighth season with the 49ers that fall. On September 11, 1994, one month before his 33rd birthday, Steve faced Joe Montana in a game for the first time since Joe left San Francisco. The game was billed as Joe versus Steve. Football fans couldn't wait!

The game was played at Arrowhead Stadium, in Kansas City. There was nothing the screaming Kansas City fans wanted more than to see Joe win this one against his old team, and he did. Although Steve played better than Joe during the first half, a couple of 49er offensive linemen were injured in the second half. Without them to protect him, Steve had to throw quickly to avoid being sacked. He threw two interceptions in the second half and Kansas City won, 24–17. The Chiefs cheered as they watched Joe leave the stadium holding the game ball.

Steve didn't make excuses for himself when he talked to reporters. "I learned from the master, and today, the master had a little more to teach the student," Steve modestly told reporters.

Steve didn't tell the reporters how disappointed he was feeling after that game. He hid his true feelings, but he did no such thing the following month. On October 2, 1994, the 49ers trailed Philadelphia, 33–8, with 4:09 minutes left in the third quarter. The game looked hopeless, and Steve was taking some brutal hits on the field. Coach Seifert

Sunday, after their names were called before the game, some of the 49ers stood between the goalposts. They wanted to block the Cowboys from running onto the Texas Stadium field when their names were announced.

As it turned out, when the game started, the 49ers couldn't stop the Cowboys from scoring between those goalposts. The Cowboys took a 28–7 halftime lead.

Early in the third quarter, the knee of a 300-pound 49er player smacked into Troy's helmet. Troy left the game with a concussion. The Cowboys' second-string quarterback, Bernie Kosar, took over. He did not give up Dallas' lead.

Steve was sacked four times. He had trouble passing because the Cowboys rushed him into throwing the ball quickly. He completed 27 of 45 passes, for 287 yards. Troy completed all but 4 of his 18 passes, for 177 yards.

Coach Johnson was correct in his prediction. The Cowboys beat the 49ers, 38–21. Then they beat Buffalo in the Super Bowl.

Steve's life went on. Three months later, he finished law school. On April 22, 1994, Steve's family watched him receive his law degree from Brigham Young University. It had taken Steve six years to complete his studies. Steve told Scott Ostler of the *San Francisco Chronicle* that he felt better about himself as a lawyer than he did as a football player. "I see that I can do a lot more good with people as a lawyer than I can . . . affect their

Steve used some of his free time to visit a homeless shelter the week before Christmas. He wore a Santa Claus hat and handed out a gift to every child there. He autographed whatever the children wanted. He also started a children's charity called "Forever Young."

After Christmas, the 49ers played one more regular-season game, against the Philadelphia Eagles. The 49ers lost, 37–34, in overtime, but Steve threw for 165 yards. When those yards were added to the other yards Steve had thrown that season, the total came to 4,023! That was a San Francisco team record. No one had thrown for more than 4,000 yards in a season — not even Joe Montana!

The NFC Championship Game was scheduled for January 23, 1994, in Dallas. For the second year in a row, it was Steve's 49ers against Troy's Cowboys.

Dallas running back Emmitt Smith wrote in his autobiography, *The Emmitt Zone*, that his coach, Jimmy Johnson, wanted to stir things up. Emmitt implied that Jimmy didn't want this repeat match-up to be boring.

Three nights before the game, Coach Johnson called a local Dallas radio station, whose talk-show host had been discussing the upcoming game on the air.

Coach Johnson made a prediction to the talk-show host and his listeners. "We will win the ballgame," Jimmy bragged, "and we're going to beat [the 49ers'] rear ends."

Coach Johnson's boast made the 49ers angry. On

After the Tampa Bay game, offensive lineman Harris Barton thought Steve was a "much better quarterback than earlier, even better than last year." Harris thought Steve was actually having a good time out on the football field!

"I think he finally just relaxed and let things happen naturally," Harris said.

As Steve was throwing all those touchdowns, he didn't forget the things that were most important to him, like his family. For example, if he had the chance, he would call his family from the sideline during a game. In fact, Steve had *many* chances that season, because the 49ers often jumped to an early lead against the other teams. When they did, the coach would pull Steve from the game to give Steve's backup, Elvis Grbac, a chance to play.

Once pulled from the game, Steve would look for a phone on the sidelines. At NFL games, the phones are usually used for players to talk to their coaches, who are watching the action from a booth up above. The coaches can give the players advice about the game.

During a game, television football commentator John Madden once saw Steve dialing a telephone on the sidelines. "That's a real phone!" Mr. Madden exclaimed. "What's he doing, calling his mother?"

Just then, the phone rang in the Youngs' house in Greenwich. Mr. Madden had guessed correctly!

In addition to his family, Steve cared a good deal about people less fortunate than he, particularly children.

7

OUT OF THE SHADOW

When the 1993 season began, Joe Montana was miles away from San Francisco, wearing a Kansas City uniform. Without Joe around, Steve had changed. Jerry Rice was asked by Frank Cooney of the *San Francisco Examiner* to describe what it was about Steve that was different. "Confidence is the word that comes to mind," Jerry said.

As an athlete plays more games and becomes more experienced, he often grows more confident. Steve was more experienced in 1993. It was his seventh year with the Niners, and his third year as their starting quarterback.

San Francisco tight end Brent Jones thought Steve could now run the Niner offense in his sleep. Steve had a good sense of where his receivers would be as he stood in the pocket with his arm cocked, ready to throw.

A case in point was a game against Tampa Bay on November 14. Steve threw four touchdowns. Afterward, he said, "I knew where people were without looking." Steve had thrown four touchdowns only once before. During the 1993 season, he threw four touchdowns in a game three times!

Dallas, Joe felt impatient at being Steve's backup. It had been two seasons since he had been injured and Steve had stepped into the starting role. Joe asked for permission to leave. On April 7, 1993, the 49ers told Joe they would allow him to talk to other teams.

On April 16th, Joe announced that he wanted to join the Kansas City Chiefs. Although the 49ers had given him permission to talk to other teams, they panicked and offered to return Joe to his starting role. This would have meant that Steve would become the backup quarterback again. Fortunately for Steve, Joe didn't accept the 49ers' new offer. He said he was definitely going to join the Chiefs.

Some of the San Francisco fans were angry that the 49ers let Joe go, especially when Steve's start in the NFC Championship Game ended in defeat against Dallas. Bill Bedwell was a typical angry fan. He thought the 49ers should have traded Steve and kept Joe. Mr. Bedwell was quoted in an article in the *Los Angeles Times* magazine as saying that Steve was a "mellow man, a gentle man, a confident man. But he A-I-N-'T Joe."

Maybe not yet. But Steve soon would be.

yards in all. He couldn't get two first downs that he needed, and two offensive drives ended without a touchdown.

Dallas held the lead throughout the game. Steve threw two interceptions, but he didn't give up. He desperately tried to help the 49ers come back. With about four-and-a-half minutes left in the game, Steve threw a touchdown pass to Jerry that cut the Cowboys' lead to 24–20. It wasn't enough. Dallas scored again with 3:43 left and beat San Francisco, 30–20.

The numbers from that game clearly show that Steve played almost as well as Cowboy quarterback Troy Aikman did. Steve completed about the same number of passes for about the same number of yards (25 of 35 passes, for 313 yards; Troy completed 24 of 35 passes, for 322 yards). Steve threw one touchdown and Troy threw two. Troy threw no interceptions, though. Those two interceptions really hurt San Francisco.

Steve walked away from the stadium in the rain. Security guards didn't have to keep the crowds away from him. The fans just stared at Steve in silence. Finally, two people shouted encouraging words to Steve. He said thank you.

Steve passed a man cleaning up the Candlestick Park stadium. "One day, you can fill Joe's shoes," the clean-up man told Steve.

While Steve was disappointed after the loss to

only when an offensive play wasn't working and it was absolutely necessary for him to run.

During that 1992 season, Steve brought the 49ers from behind three times. He led the 49ers to a 14–2 record.

Steve played so well that his numbers showed that he was the best passer in the league that season. He threw the most touchdowns (25) and the fewest interceptions (7). He also completed the highest percentage of passes thrown (66.7). The National Football League honored Steve with its Most Valuable Player award. Steve also was awarded the Player of the Year award by *Sports Illustrated*, and he received a 49er team award for being the 49ers' most inspirational and courageous player.

On January 9, 1993, San Francisco played the Washington Redskins in the NFC playoffs. Steve started in his first post-season game. Although he was nervous, Steve threw two touchdowns, as San Francisco won, 20–13. It was on to the NFC championship!

At the beginning of the championship game, against the Dallas Cowboys on January 17, 1993, it looked as if Steve was on a roll. On just the third play of the game, Steve hit Jerry Rice with what looked like a 63-yard touchdown pass. But a referee called a 49er guard for holding, and the touchdown was taken back.

"That may have been the turning point," Steve said later on.

For the rest of the first half, Steve threw for just 63

It wasn't easy for Steve to play when he knew some of his teammates didn't have faith in him, but he kept on playing. "I didn't want to walk away from it," Steve said. "I could have, but I didn't want to."

During an October 3 game against the Atlanta Falcons, Steve threw a *97-yard* touchdown pass to John Taylor. It was a team record! Then Steve injured his knee in that same game and missed the next five games. Despite that, Steve led the NFL in passing for the 1991 season. He won several awards for his achievements.

The San Francisco fans still liked Joe better than Steve and said so to the press. Steve's father and his agent, Leigh Steinberg, thought Steve should leave the 49ers and join a different team.

Steve refused. It would be too easy for him to give up. Steve wasn't a quitter. Even though he knew Joe was a better quarterback, Steve was determined to become the best San Francisco ever had.

During the 1992 season, Steve had more playing time, and he improved as a result. He calmed down and waited an extra second for his receivers to get open before deciding whether to pass or run. He became more aware of where his receivers were, and which one was his best target.

If the 49er receivers were too heavily guarded, then Steve would run. He would sprint forward, with his eyes focused ahead. He would still be looking to pass, moving with his arm cocked, ready to throw. Now Steve scrambled ter, with the 49ers behind, 15–13. Steve completed one pass, but by game's end, the score had not changed.

At the beginning of the 1991 season, Joe needed surgery on his elbow. He would miss the season. Coach Seifert named Steve the new starting quarterback. Finally, Steve would have a chance to play!

Play he did. On September 22, 1991, the Los Angeles Rams led San Francisco, 10–3, with just 41 seconds remaining in the first half of the game. Steve did something Joe would have done. In 23 seconds, he moved the 49ers 65 yards for a touchdown. His 12-yard pass to John Taylor put San Francisco back in the game, which they ended up winning, 27–10.

"That felt good," Steve admitted afterward.

A week later, on September 29, 1991, the 49ers played the Los Angeles Raiders. The 49ers were losing again. They were trailing by 6 points when Steve brought his team to the Raider's 19-yard line. The score was 12–6, and all Steve needed to do was complete his fourth-down pass to keep the drive going. With 1 minute 48 seconds remaining on the clock, Steve's pass fell to the ground, incomplete. San Francisco lost.

In the locker room, San Francisco pass rusher Charles Haley cursed Steve. He punched his fist through a wall and then fell onto the ground, weeping. Charles was used to having Joe there to pull off last-second wins.

STEVE YOUNG 47

January 22, 1989, Steve watched from the sideline as Joe won his third Super Bowl for the 49ers. San Francisco beat Cincinnati, 20–16.

After the Super Bowl, Steve began his first semester at BYU law school. He knew that he would not play football forever. Steve wanted to become a lawyer like his dad one day. Steve attended law school one semester a year, during the NFL off-season. It would take him six years to graduate.

Reporters wondered why a millionaire like Steve would care about studying law. "My father made me," Steve joked.

That same month, Bill Walsh retired as head coach of the 49ers. He left to become a football analyst on TV. San Francisco defensive coordinator George Seifert replaced him.

Steve started three games during the 1989 season, and played a little bit in Super Bowl XXIV, on January 28, 1990. It was really Joe's day. He threw five touchdown passes, a Super Bowl record, as San Francisco crushed the Denver Broncos, 55–10. Steve now owned two Super Bowl rings. Neither one meant anything much to him.

Steve started in only one game during the 1990 season, after which the Niners had a 14–2 record. They advanced to the NFC Championship Game but lost to the New York Giants. Joe broke a finger on his throwing hand during that game. Steve stepped in during the fourth quar-

Vikings were ahead, 21–10, when Steve launched a 78-yard touchdown pass to San Francisco receiver John Taylor.

San Francisco still trailed by four. With a little more than two minutes left to play, Steve ran onto the field to lead another San Francisco drive.

The score was 21–17. The ball was on the Viking 49-yard line. Steve took the snap and surprised everyone when he tucked the ball under his arm and ran.

Three Minnesota linemen lunged for Steve . . . and missed! Eight Minnesota defenders couldn't stop him! Steve raced toward the goalposts and dove into the end zone with the ball.

The crowd went crazy! This wasn't something they were likely to see Joe do. It was a truly amazing run. When the NFL celebrated its 75th anniversary six years later, the league chose that run as the best run in football history! Steve's run beat out runs by some of the NFL's most famous running backs.

It may have been historic, but Steve's run didn't persuade his coaches to give him more playing time. On

HEAD TO HEAD

Steve won his first NFL Most Valuable Player award in 1992. Troy won his first Super Bowl, and the Super Bowl MVP award two years later.

before. He walked over to Joe during the third quarter and said, "I'm going with Steve."

Coach Walsh benched Joe, and Joe was furious! Steve stepped in, rushed for a game-high 72 yards, and scored on a five-yard run. The 49ers still lost.

Joe accused Steve of begging their coach for more playing time. He told the *Washington Post* that Steve was "on a big push for himself."

You would think Steve would get angry and tell Joe off, but he didn't. "I don't feel any anger. I just don't," Steve commented in the *Los Angeles Times*.

Joe was not always nice to Steve, which made it difficult for Steve to enjoy playing for the team. There were some mornings when Steve didn't want to get out of bed or go to practice. When Steve finally arrived at the stadium on those mornings, he wanted to turn around and go home.

Joe wasn't the only player Steve had trouble with. Jerry Rice didn't like working with Steve because he had trouble catching Steve's passes. Steve is left-handed, and the passes he threw had a different spin to them. Steve would also throw a split-second too late. Jerry felt that Joe's passes were perfectly timed and had a good arc.

Steve needed more practice and more game time. Then he would play better.

He did. On October 30, 1988, Steve played his best game yet. Steve started in place of Joe, who had injured his back. The 49ers were playing the Minnesota Vikings. The

6

IN JOE'S SHADOW

A writer from *Sports Illustrated* asked Joe Montana this question: Do you have any advice for Steve Young, your backup quarterback?

"Yeah," Joe said. "Break a leg."

Was Joe smiling when he said that? The writer wasn't sure.

It wasn't easy for Joe to welcome Steve to the team. Joe was 31 years old, but he wasn't ready to quit playing football. Steve was five years younger and healthy. Steve wanted to take over from Joe as the starter, but Joe wanted to stay put.

Joe was a hero in San Francisco. He had won Super Bowls in 1982 and 1985. He had helped the 49ers come from behind many times to win games. He could even turn a game around when only a few seconds remained on the clock.

Not always, though. Joe couldn't find a way to win a 1987 playoff game against Minnesota. The 49ers were losing, and Coach Walsh did something he had never done

Bucs won just four games out of 32. Steve didn't help. In his two seasons, Steve won just 3 of the 19 games he started.

Tampa Bay gave up on Steve Young and prepared to recruit University of Miami Heisman Trophy winner Vinny Testaverde.

Meanwhile, San Francisco coach Bill Walsh thought Steve had talent. Coach Walsh thought he could develop the quarterback's skills.

On April 24, 1987, Tampa Bay traded Steve to the 49ers in exchange for two 1987 draft picks. Steve was excited to be joining the 49ers. He felt that Coach Walsh was the best coach around, especially in teaching quarterbacks. He also wanted to play for a contending team in a city with mild weather.

Steve's role with the 49ers would be as back-up to Joe Montana. Joe had joined the team eight years earlier and had won Super Bowls in 1982 and '85.

Joe was getting older and missing playing time because of injuries. Bill looked to Steve as the 49er quarterback of the future. When Steve arrived in San Francisco, he would discover how true that was.

like a rookie. His coach, Leeman Bennett, wanted Steve to be an old-style quarterback who took the snap, dropped back, and passed.

That wasn't Steve's style. His first instinct was still to run. He ran even though he had a receiver who was open to receive his pass. One reason that Steve ran was because the Bucs weren't that good at protecting him while he passed. Too often, Steve had to hurry and throw, causing him to throw bad passes. As he had with the Express, he threw more interceptions than touchdowns. Steve competed for playing time with the Buccaneers' other quarterback, Steve DeBerg. Steve DeBerg had more experience playing with the Bucs and other NFL teams. Even so, Tampa Bay won just 2 out of 16 games that season.

Tampa Bay didn't win any more games in 1986 than it had in 1985. Fans threw lemons onto the field during the final home game of the 1986 season.

In the two seasons Steve played for Tampa Bay, the

HEAD TO HEAD

On September 10, 1985, when Steve was 23, he became an NFL quarterback, joining the Tampa Bay Buccaneers. Troy was a sophomore at the University of Oklahoma and the Sooners' starting quarterback.

Celtics right in the middle of an Express game against the Denver Gold!

Steve was a basketball fan and kept looking up from the huddle to see what Magic Johnson or Larry Bird would do next. The Lakers won, 109–102. The Express lost.

On the way to the last game of the 1985 season, the driver of the team bus pulled over to the side of the road. He refused to drive the Express team any further. "I'm not moving until I get paid," he said.

The team passed around a hat, collected money, and paid him. After that, there wasn't a team bus anymore. Steve and the other players would joke, "Okay, whose Mom has the car pool this week?"

The Express won 3 out of 18 games that season. Steve finished his two years with 16 touchdown passes and 22 interceptions.

Steve now wanted to join the NFL. He knew that the Tampa Bay Buccaneers needed a good quarterback and wanted him. Unfortunately, Tampa Bay was one of the worst teams in the NFL. *Maybe* Steve could help turn them into a winning team!

Steve paid the Los Angeles Express $1.2 million dollars to get out of his contract. On September 10, 1985, he signed a new contract with Tampa, becoming the 13th starting quarterback in the Bucs' 10-year history.

In his first season with his new team, Steve played

the New Jersey Generals. His team lost, 26–10.

In the middle of April, playing against the Memphis Showboats, Steve threw an 81-yard-touchdown pass. That was the longest pass in the USFL that year, and Steve's touchdown helped Los Angeles beat Memphis, 23–17, in overtime!

On April 20, the Express played the Chicago Blitz. Steve became the first player in professional football history to pass for 300 yards and rush for 100 yards in the same game. Despite Steve's amazing performance, the Express lost, 49–29.

Steve was a million-dollar quarterback, but he hadn't changed his living style. He still drove around in the 1965 Oldsmobile his father had given him in college, wore shirts and socks with holes in them, and ate at Burger King.

Meanwhile, Mr. Oldenburg could not pay all of his team's expenses. In July 1984, Mr. Oldenburg gave up the team to the other USFL team owners.

When the 1985 season began, the new owners also had problems paying the team's bills. One day, a big truck pulled up to the team office. Steve watched as moving men hauled out the office furniture.

No one cared much about the games anymore. During one of the last games of the 1985 season, the Express operations manager put the NBA finals on the DiamondVision big-screen television inside the stadium. What few fans there were could watch the Lakers and the

Steve, Mr. Steinberg, and Mr. Oldenburg kept on arguing about the terms of the deal. Later that night, Mr. Oldenburg walked over to Steve and jabbed him in the chest. "You're never going to make more money than this," he said.

Steve didn't care how much money Mr. Oldenburg was offering. "If you touch me one more time, I'll deck you," Steve said. Steve and his agent were escorted out of the office.

Three days later, on March 5, Steve signed with the Express. The media called 22-year-old Steve "The $40 Million Dollar Man." *The New York Times* even printed a cartoon of a football center hiking bags of money to Steve!

Many people criticized Steve for being greedy. That made Steve sad. Steve told Michael Janofsky of *The New York Times* that he wanted to be a sports hero and do the right things. "I want some mom somewhere to say: 'Grow up and be like this guy,'" Steve said.

The USFL was a spring league. The Express's season had started on February 28, before Steve had even signed his contract. To join his team, Steve had to leave BYU before he graduated. (He would complete his studies and graduate from BYU the following December.)

When Steve arrived in Los Angeles the second week in March, the team was 0–2. Because Steve had missed training camp, he didn't start his first game until April 1. Steve threw one touchdown and one interception against the Dallas Cowboys. He had heard about Steve's offer from the USFL. Roger told Steve that the money wasn't worth it, that it would be better for Steve to take less money and play in the NFL. The NFL was a league that had been around for a long time and would continue to be around for a long time. The USFL was only two years old at that time.

That night, Steve and his agent met with Mr. Oldenburg again. They were nervous about the league being new. They wanted to make sure Steve would be paid, and paid well, for joining the new league, and not the NFL. Steve and Mr. Steinberg wanted Steve to receive money up-front as a guarantee that Mr. Oldenburg would live up to his word in the contract. That made Mr. Oldenburg angry. (The fact that it was his birthday and he was missing his party arguing over this contract did not help matters.) Mr. Oldenburg wadded up a bunch of bills and threw them at Steve's feet.

"Here's all the guarantees you'll need," Mr. Oldenburg growled.

HEAD TO HEAD

Troy was still a senior in high school in March 1984, when Steve signed a $40 million contract to play for the L.A. Express in the new United States Football League.

back. Ken had taken Cincinnati to the Super Bowl two years earlier. Ken was likely to remain as Cincinnati's starter for several years to come. And Steve didn't want to be anyone's backup.

J. William Oldenburg was the owner of the Express. Mr. Oldenburg knew that Steve could help his new team. If he could get a top-notch college player like Steve to join his team, more fans than ever before would buy tickets to Express games.

Mr. Oldenburg decided to make sure Steve would sign with his team. The Express drafted Gordon Hudson, Steve's buddy from BYU, and then Steve. Next, Mr. Oldenburg invited Steve and his agent, Leigh Steinberg, to fly out to the West Coast to meet him and discuss Steve's contract with the team.

Mr. Oldenburg always did things in a flashy way. When Steve arrived at Mr. Oldenburg's office, on February 21, he looked up at an electric sign. It blinked the words: STEVE YOUNG, MR. BYU, MR. UTAH, MR. EVERYTHING.

Then Mr. Oldenburg made his offer: If Steve would play for the Los Angeles Express, Mr. Oldenburg would pay him $40 million dollars. Of course, Steve wouldn't receive the money all at once. He would receive it over many years, all the way to the year 2027, when Steve turned 65!

Mr. Oldenburg gave Steve and his agent time to think it over. On March 2, Steve received a call from his boyhood hero, Roger Staubach. Roger had been the quarterback for

5

A DIFFERENT PATH TO THE PROS

At 4 A.M., Steve received a phone call in his hotel room. Steve was in Hawaii to play in the Hula Bowl with the best college seniors in the country. However, the caller wasn't interested in the Hula Bowl.

The caller was the head trainer and scout for the Los Angeles Express. The Express was one of 12 teams in a new football league called the United States Football League (USFL).

It was January 4, 1984, and the USFL draft was being held that morning. The caller wanted to know if Steve would play in the USFL. Or would he only play in the NFL?

Steve said he would consider the USFL. Steve knew if he played in the NFL, he would probably have to join the Cincinnati Bengals. The Bengals wanted him, and the Bengals had the first pick in the 1984 draft coming up in May. Steve wasn't sure that he wanted to play for the Bengals. Ken Anderson was the Bengals' starting quarter-

There was one more thing Steve needed and that was a victory at the Holiday Bowl. "My dad says he'll buy me new tires if we win the Holiday Bowl," Steve told Dave Distel of *The Los Angeles Times*.

On December 19, BYU played Missouri in the Holiday Bowl, in San Diego. There were 30 seconds left in the game, and Missouri led BYU by 1 point. The Cougars had the ball on third down with one yard to go.

BYU receiver coach Norm Chow wanted Steve to hand off to running back Eddie Stinnett, who would sweep to the right. Steve was supposed to keep on running toward the goal line and surprise the Missouri defense when Eddie threw the ball back to him. The play worked! Steve caught the ball, crossed the goal line, and ran around like a little kid. The Cougars won! Steve was BYU's hero.

Steve didn't need his father to buy him new tires. He was about to earn a lot of money in the NFL. Steve and Gordon wanted to stay together. "We're thinking about telling the pros that we're a package deal," Gordon told *Sports Illustrated*. "Can't have one without the other."

Steve and Gordon got their wish in the 1983 draft. Down the line, however, things didn't turn out the way they expected.

quoted in *Sports Illustrated* as saying that he thought Steve was the best quarterback BYU had ever had. "And he's the most accurate passer I've ever seen. Period," he stated.

And to think that Steve came from a high school football team that didn't pass!

Steve had done more in college than just play football. He majored in two subjects, finance and international relations. His grades were so good that he was chosen as an academic All-America. That meant that Steve was one of the best athletes in the nation *and* an excellent student. Steve was also one of 11 college football seniors to receive the National Football Foundation and Hall of Fame Division I-A scholar-athlete award.

The biggest honor Steve could receive at the end of his BYU football career would be the Heisman Trophy, awarded to the top college football player in the nation. The winner is chosen by two groups: athletes who won the trophy in the past and members of the media. The trophy is named after John W. Heisman, who, in 1917, coached Georgia Tech to the national football championship. For Steve, it was not to be. On December 3, the trophy went to Nebraska running back Mike Rozier. Steve finished second in the voting, but being the Heisman Trophy runner-up was a great honor in itself. Steve won more votes than Jim McMahon, who had finished third in the voting for the 1981 Heisman Trophy, two years before.

career-high 486 yards during BYU's 46–28 win.

Steve played his final regular season home game against the University of Utah. Sixty-five-thousand fans cheered Steve and the Cougars that day. The crowd went wild as Steve completed all but three of 25 passes, of which six went for touchdowns. Final score: 55–7. When Steve took his final bow, the BYU fans applauded him loudly.

BYU coaches had wondered who could replace Jim McMahon. Now the question was, who could replace Steve Young?

Steve and Gordon had been selected for every All-America team. Both set many NCAA records. Steve completed more passes in a season than any other quarterback (306). He achieved the highest percentage of completed passes (71.3 percent). He gained the most offensive yards per game (395.1). Steve passed for 3,902 yards. His 4,346 passing and running yards topped the nation that year. Steve tied or broke 13 NCAA records.

A Dallas Cowboy college scout named Gil Brandt was

HEAD TO HEAD

In November 1983, Steve was 22 and the runner-up for the Heisman Trophy. Troy was a 17-year-old senior quarterback on his high shool varsity football team in Henryetta, Oklahoma.

Mr. Young told Steve he would drive the car across the country and leave it with him.

Steve groaned. "It'll never make it," Steve told his father. He knew the car had more than 200,000 miles on it. It really should have been resting in peace on a junk heap.

The car *did* make it across the country, and Steve grew fond of it. He often drove that car to the local 7-Eleven, where he could buy three hot dogs for a dollar. Steve was also a hungry quarterback.

No one expected BYU to do well during the 1983 season, Steve's senior year. Several good players were gone. The Cougars lost their first game of the season to Baylor University in Waco, Texas. The score was 40–36, which BYU linebacker Todd Shell was particularly unhappy about. "Todd, don't worry about a thing," Steve said. "We won't lose another game the rest of the year."

Steve was right! Steve and Gordon connected many times to help BYU win all of its remaining games.

"Maybe it's just because we know each other so well, but I can always feel what Steve's gonna do and he can feel what I'll do," Gordon told Teri Thompson of the *Rocky Mountain News*. "It's like he reads my mind."

In BYU's 63–28 romp over Bowling Green, Steve passed for five touchdowns and ran for two more. When BYU played Air Force, Steve completed 18 consecutive passes for an NCAA single-game record! He threw a him."

At the end of Steve's sophomore year, Jim graduated and joined the Chicago Bears. This meant that the next fall, Steve would be named BYU's new starting quarterback!

When Steve began his junior year in the fall of 1982, Ted Tollner left BYU to coach at another school. Mike Holmgren replaced him.

Like Ted Tollner, Coach Holmgren felt Steve had talent. "Steve Young has great physical ability, an excellent arm, tremendous foot speed and running ability," Coach Holmgren told the BYU student newspaper, the *Daily Universe*. "He's an intelligent, intense young man, and I think all he needs to be a great player is a chance to be a great player."

With more game experience that junior year, Steve developed into one of the best college passers in the nation. Steve gained a sense of when to stay in the pocket and when to throw. He rarely made a bad pass.

Steve completed 22 passes in a row over two games, setting an NCAA record. He threw for 3,100 yards and 18 touchdowns. BYU won its seventh Western Athletic Conference (WAC) championship, and the WAC named Steve its Offensive Player of the Year.

Steve lived off campus his junior year and felt he needed a car. He called his father one day and asked him if he could help him buy one. Mr. Young offered Steve his 1965 Oldsmobile.

"I got some breaks," Steve said. "I might be a defensive back today if [Coach] Tollner hadn't been hired."

Steve began to relax and feel more comfortable now that Coach Scovil was gone. Steve was a perfectionist, and he was determined to be the best quarterback there. He threw the ball about 200 times during practice. He threw so much his arm got sore!

Steve's hard work paid off, and his passing improved during the spring of his freshman year. He played better in scrimmages against his teammates. One of the quarterbacks who had been better than Steve began to play worse. At the junior-varsity awards banquet that spring, Steve was named BYU's most valuable player.

It was no wonder Steve was excited when he began his sophomore year in the fall of 1981. He had been chosen to be Jim McMahon's backup. When Jim injured his knee during a game against Colorado, Steve stepped in. On his first series, Steve completed a 27-yard pass, scrambled for a 29-yard run, and threw an 11-yard touchdown pass to his friend Gordon. BYU beat Colorado, 44–20!

Steve put a lot of pressure on himself to be the next Jim McMahon. "I told him he didn't have to be," Coach Edwards said. "All we wanted him to do was be as good as he could be, and that would be good enough to be Brigham Young's quarterback. He is such a gifted athlete; turning the corner, he can really accelerate as people are closing on come home. Mr. Young told Steve that he could quit the team, but he couldn't come home.

"I don't live with quitters," Mr. Young said.

Steve stayed, but things got worse before they got better. "We might have to move you to another position," Coach Edwards told Steve. Mr. Edwards wanted Steve to play defense.

Steve got a break when Coach Scovil decided to leave BYU and coach at San Diego State University. After Coach Scovil left, two of the freshman quarterbacks who were rated higher than Steve decided to attend a different school.

BYU's new quarterback coach was a man named Ted Tollner. Coach Tollner was running laps around the BYU indoor track one day and saw Steve practicing his throws. Coach Tollner thought Steve had a nice release on the ball. Being noticed by Coach Tollner was important for Steve.

HEAD TO HEAD

On the NCAA list of all-time leaders in passing efficiency, Steve ranks third. (He is behind two other BYU quarterbacks, Ty Detmer and Jim McMahon!) That ranking is for 500-or-more completions. On the list for fewer than 500 completions, Troy Aikman is third.

Steve had a difficult time adjusting to college. He was homesick, and his family was now 3,000 miles away. Having the name Young and a statue of his great-great-great-grandfather on campus didn't help. Steve still missed his family, and he still couldn't throw a good pass.

Steve was the eighth-string quarterback his freshman year. BYU had so many quarterbacks that the football team didn't really need Steve, especially since he didn't have that much experience passing the ball.

When Steve arrived at the school, Jim McMahon was BYU's all-American star quarterback. And 1980 would turn out to be a spectacular year for Jim. He threw for 4,571 yards, more than any other college quarterback. With Jim as their starting quarterback, the Cougars lost only two games. Jim would break 55 National Collegiate Athletic Association records and tie another before his college career was over.

The varsity team was in Jim's skilled hands. Steve played on the BYU junior varsity team that freshman year. The BYU offensive coordinator, Doug Scovil, didn't think much of Steve as a quarterback. He didn't think Steve was valuable to the team. That's why Coach Scovil asked Steve to run the next opponent's offense during practice, and watch the games from the stands. Steve wasn't even asked to wear his uniform on game days.

Steve was miserable. He called his father and told him that he wanted to quit playing football, leave BYU, and

4

WAITING IN THE WINGS

When Steve arrived at Brigham Young University in the fall of 1980, he joined the football team with another freshman named Gordon Hudson. Gordon was a tight end. (A tight end is usally big and strong. He can catch passes and block on running plays.) Gordon noticed that Steve was wearing some weird, high-topped sneakers. He watched as Steve took a snap, dropped back to pass, tripped, and fell. Gordon started to laugh.

"I said to myself, 'What is this guy, a walk-on?'" Gordon told *Sports Illustrated*. (Walk-ons are players who are not recruited to play a sport for a school, nor are they offered scholarships. Instead, when they arrive at the school, they "walk on" to the field to try out for the team.) Gordon remembers thinking that Steve looked "ridiculous."

In spite of this beginning, Steve and Gordon went on to become best friends. They teamed up to be the best quarterback-to-tight-end passing combination in the nation. But on that first day of practice, you would never know Steve could throw a football.

Members of the Mormon church, which is also called the Church of Jesus Christ of Latter Day Saints, do not believe in smoking or drinking alcohol or even caffeine. People liked Steve and respected him the way he was. He was intelligent, polite, sincere, and hard-working. He also had a good sense of humor and was fun to be around.

"I look back in high school and I had a ball," Steve told the *Rocky Mountain News*. "I can't imagine anyone having more fun than I did."

When it came time to choose a college, Steve chose Brigham Young University. His father had gone there, and the school was affiliated with the Mormon church. BYU has an excellent football program. Steve knew he would receive a very good education on a beautiful campus.

There was just one problem. It had to do with the style of football played by the Brigham Young University Cougars. They had one of the best passing teams in the country. Greenwich had been anything but a passing team. Steve knew he was going to be challenged if he joined the Cougar football team, and he was right!

Lowe wouldn't give Steve a break, even though he coached the water polo and boys' swim teams and knew how tough it was to play sports and do well in school.

"I don't care about football," Mr. Lowe would tell Steve. "Sports are great, but sports aren't life."

Mr. Lowe cared about how Steve did in school. Steve worked hard. He brought his C up to an A, and he respected Mr. Lowe for being tough on him. He would often stop by to talk to Mr. Lowe.

Mr. Lowe didn't realize it at the time, but he was a great influence on Steve. Sixteen years later, Steve nominated Mr. Lowe for the National Football League 1994 Teacher of the Year Award. Mr. Lowe won!

When football season ended, Steve began playing basketball. He was 6' 1" and captain of the team. He averaged about 15 points per game at forward. In the spring, Steve captained the baseball team. He was an outstanding pitcher.

"He would just throw the ball across the plate and he'd get everybody out," said his friend and teammate, Randy Caravella. Steve pitched a few no-hitters, including one the day after the senior prom had been held. Steve also played centerfield.

Going to school, playing three sports, and attending religious school classes kept Steve very busy. He would get up each weekday morning at 5 A.M. Then he would attend a 6 A.M. religious school class at his Mormon church.

35-yard pass with less than a minute left to play. Steve rushed for 194 yards and two touchdowns that day. Steve loved hearing the Greenwich High School band play the Cardinal fight song after he ran the ball in for his touchdowns, and he *really* enjoyed hearing it more than once in a game!

The Cardinals finished the season with a 7–3 record, but lost the Fairfield County championship on Thanksgiving Day to Darien. Steve tried his best to help his team, but the Cardinals couldn't score even one touchdown. Steve went home disappointed after the 17–0 loss.

Steve's rushing yards are near the top of the Greenwich High School all-time list, which is unusual for a quarterback. Steve ran for 1,928 yards, a number good enough for second place. He threw for 1,220 yards. Steve's younger brother Mike topped that by 200 yards when *he* became the Greenwich High School quarterback. Steve has yet to live that down.

Despite all the time he spent playing football, Steve was an A student and was elected to the National Honor Society. Steve earned only one C in high school, in mathematics. It was in advanced-placement calculus his senior year. (Advanced-placement courses allow you to earn extra credits for college.)

"Mr. Lowe, I play football. Give me a break," Steve would say to his mathematics teacher, Terry Lowe. Mr.

this quarterback who ran like a fullback.

One day, a high school football player from the neighboring town of Stamford called his cousin, who was a student at Greenwich High School. "You better warn your buddy," he said threateningly. "I'm going to put him out of the game."

The Greenwich High School player just laughed. "You've got to catch him first," he said.

The Stamford player didn't. In fact, few opposing players could. They didn't know how to defend against Steve. Because he was so good at running with the ball, opponents had to block Steve's run rather than his pass.

"All he needed was the tiniest little hole, and Steve found a way to get through it and pick up a few yards," said Steve's co-captain, Mike Gasparino, to a reporter from the *Greenwich Time*. "No [defender] ever really got a good shot at Steve." Some opposing teams were forced to assign two people to cover him.

Steve ran because he was too embarrassed to throw. "It was something I didn't want to do in public," Steve told Teri Thompson of the *Rocky Mountain News*. Luckily, the Cardinals weren't a passing team.

Steve turned 18 during the fall of 1979. It was his senior year and he co-captained the team. During that season, Steve helped the Cardinals come from behind to beat Stamford Catholic. He threw the winning touchdown on a because the quarterback "draws" the defense toward him, and then runs.) Steve completed seven of nine passes. He helped the Cardinals shut down Ridgefield High School, 27–0. Steve won player-of-the-week honors, voted by coaches and teammates.

Steve's great strength was his ability to sense what the opposing defense would do. He could judge whether his opponents would try to cover his team man-to-man, for example, or try a quarterback blitz. (The blitz is an all-out rush by the defense toward the quarterback to prevent him from throwing the ball.) In the case of a blitz, Steve was able to run so fast he could avoid the blitz and gain a first down or a touchdown by himself. Defensive backs were always looking at the back of Steve's uniform. Steve flew past safeties before they even moved.

"There've been a lot of guys who could throw the ball," Coach Ornato told Mr. Lupica. "How many of them could throw it the way he [could in high school], and run like a Thoroughbred?"

Not many. Opposing teams were determined to stop

HEAD TO HEAD

When Steve graduated from Greenwich High School, in Connecticut, at age 18, Troy was a 13-year-old eighth-grader in Henryetta, Oklahoma.

Ornato was discouraged when the junior varsity team — his team of the future — won only one game that fall. Steve was the jay-vee quarterback, and he wasn't very good. He threw eight interceptions in one game! He surely didn't look like a future Super Bowl quarterback.

Playing on a weak team and not doing well himself didn't stop Steve from wanting to be the starting quarterback on the varsity team the next year. But Coach Ornato had someone else in mind. He was a 6' 3" senior named Bill Barber, who could throw well.

Just before the 1978 season began, Bill hurt his shoulder. Coach Ornato asked Steve to start in a scrimmage, or practice game. More than 10 years later, when he was interviewed by sports columnist Mike Lupica, the coach was able to remember what happened next: Steve was excited and nervous. On one of his first plays, he took the snap, but dropped the ball. He just stared at the ball resting on the ground. Then he leaped into action — Steve picked up the ball and ran 75 yards for a touchdown!

"What the heck was that?" Coach Ornato recalled asking one of the other coaches. It was clear that either the opposing team didn't have much of a defense, or Greenwich High School had one heck of a quarterback.

During the first regular-season game, Steve scored a touchdown on a quarterback draw play. (In a quarterback draw, the quarterback drops back as if he were going to pass the ball. Instead, he runs with it. It's called a draw play

3

RUSHING THROUGH HIGH SCHOOL

When Steve was growing up, kids in Greenwich didn't begin high school until 10th grade. That year, if they wanted to play football, they could only play on the junior varsity team. When they were juniors (11th graders), they could move up and play for varsity coach Mike Ornato. Coach Ornato always checked over the junior varsity team so that he could see what kind of talent would be coming his way the following year.

In the fall of 1977, Coach Ornato took one look at the junior varsity team and rolled his eyes. This was the worst group of sophomores the coach had ever seen! As a group, they were too slow and too skinny.

Coach Ornato was used to winning games, not losing them. The Greenwich High School varsity team was respected around the state of Connecticut. The team name was the Cardinals, and the white football helmet with the red bird on it was something to wear with pride. So Coach

Many kids thought of North Mianus as the wrong side of town. Greenwich has a lot of wealthy residents, and it was true that Steve didn't live where the rich kids lived. It was not considered cool to grow up where Steve did.

Steve grew up thinking he was poor, but he really wasn't. Mr. Young would tell Steve and the other Young children that he made just $6 dollars a day. Mr. Young wanted his children to go out and earn money for the things they wanted, instead of expecting to get them for free from him. That way Steve and his brothers and sister would get used to working hard for the things they wanted in life.

Steve began delivering the local newspaper, the *Greenwich Time*. Little did he know that years later, he would be written about in the same paper. During the summer, he mowed lawns or dished out ice cream at a local ice cream parlor. Whatever money Steve earned, his father put in the bank. Many years later, Steve asked about the money, which had collected interest over the years. With the interest paid by the bank, Steve's savings had grown to $11,000!

Back then, Steve was growing, too. In 1977, Steve entered Greenwich High School. His football career was underway.

couldn't throw that well back then. At night, Steve looked at a picture of Roger on a poster hanging over his bed. He dreamed of playing in the NFL. Little did Steve know that his dream would come true!

Steve played many sports, too, including tennis and street hockey. He would practice hard at home and then try to show off to the other kids at school recess. One day, Steve made a shot in the Eastern Junior High School gym that made the other children laugh. Steve dribbled the length of the gym and sank a layup, right into the other team's basket! Steve was very embarrassed when he learned that he had scored two points for the other team.

In junior high school, Steve loved reading books about football players and writing school reports about them. He was an excellent student who earned high grades.

At Eastern Junior High School, kids picked on Steve because he had attended North Mianus Elementary School.

HEAD TO HEAD

Steve quarterbacked his first football team when he was an eighth grader in junior high school in Greenwich, Connecticut. Steve was 13 years old at the time. At the same time, Troy was an 8-year-old fourth-grader living in Cerritos, California.

word for "deeply embarrassed." Steve asked a referee to get his mother off the field. "After that, I became a quarterback," Steve told the *Greenwich Time*.

At Eastern Junior High School, Steve got his wish. Steve was pleased when the Eastern football coach, Joseph D'Antona, chose him as quarterback. Now he could be like his hero, Roger Staubach, then quarterback of the Dallas Cowboys.

When Steve received his football jersey on the first day of practice, he was handed one with the number 8 on it. He wanted 12, the number Roger wore. But Steve was too small and skinny for two numbers to fit side-by-side on his back.

"This isn't much of a number," Steve recalls thinking, looking disappointedly at his new football uniform. "No one wears eight. Only dummies wear eight."

Little did Steve know! Number 8 would be the number of a future Dallas quarterback named Troy Aikman. Troy would win the Super Bowl three times for the Cowboys. Steve would also be wearing number 8 in the future, when he held up the 49ers' trophy at Super Bowl XXIX!

When playing in his junior high school games, Steve tried to imitate Roger Staubach. Roger was called "Roger the Dodger," and Steve was a good runner like Roger. Steve ran so fast in junior high school that it was hard for anyone to catch up with him to tackle him. Steve had to run. He thought it looked weird because it was too curly. To cover it up and straighten it, Steve wore a ski cap. Steve's hair never did straighten out, though.

When Steve was in fifth or sixth grade, he invited a friend to sleep over at his house. Steve told his younger brother and sister that they were to stay out of his bedroom. Melissa and Mike did not listen. They took off all their clothes and ran into Steve's room, naked. They ran around the room, giggling. "We thoroughly embarrassed him for his entire childhood," Melissa told the *Greenwich Time* newspaper.

Despite all the pranks, Steve had fun with his siblings. Another brother, Jimmy, was born in 1978, while Steve was in high school.

Steve began his football career playing wide receiver in a local youth program. He learned a play called Big Red. In Big Red, the quarterback flipped the ball to Steve, who caught it and ran. The play worked many times, and Steve's team won the town championship.

During one game, a big kid grabbed Steve by the neck and tackled him to the ground. Mrs. Young ran onto the field and shook the other boy. "Don't you ever do that to my son again!" Mrs. Young scolded. She was afraid that the boy was going to hurt Steve by grabbing him around his neck and throwing him down.

Mr. Young said Steve was "mortified." That's another

Young didn't want to live in a big city like New York. They wanted a smaller town with houses rather than apartment buildings. They hoped they would find one with another nice yard. They found what they wanted in the town of Greenwich, Connecticut, 50 minutes by train from the city. In Greenwich, there were many streets with sidewalks for the children to ride their bicycles on and trees for them to climb in. There were excellent schools and sports activities, too. The Youngs bought a new house, moved in, and were very happy.

Steve loved to play with Mike and Melissa. When he was away from his family, Steve was shy. He felt uncomfortable sleeping at someone's house. He would get homesick. When Steve wanted to have a sleepover with a friend, it had to be at *his* house.

Steve was always worrying. One weekend, Mr. and Mrs. Young went away, and a couple from their church took care of the children. Steve was about 8 years old at the time and felt some doubt about the husband of the couple who was baby-sitting for them.

"Mike," Steve whispered to his younger brother. "That guy there baby-sitting us, I know he's a bank robber."

Mike wasn't as sure, but Steve called a family meeting anyway. Should they call the police? The baby-sitter wasn't really a bank robber, and the children never did call the police. But Steve worried just the same.

Steve also worried about his hair, which is black. He

he'd rather have a left-handed son than a spastic right-handed son," Steve told Eric McHugh of *Greenwich Time* newspaper.

In Salt Lake City, the Youngs lived on a street with many children. Steve loved playing all sorts of games and sports with his neighbors. Mr. Young nailed up a hoop in the backyard.

The Youngs' front-yard was perfect for playing football, and there was often a game going on. No matter how big or old the neighborhood children were, Steve insisted upon joining them. He'd run into the biggest kids on the street and try to tackle them. Every once in a while, Steve would get hurt and cry. Steve was pretty tough, though. In fact, he was one of the toughest kids in the neighborhood.

Steve was determined to succeed at whatever he did, even when he was in first or second grade. When a boy across the street learned to ride a unicycle (a bike that has only one wheel), Steve made up his mind to learn how to ride one, too. He practiced every day, wobbling and crashing for hours until he was able to ride it without falling off.

Steve said good-bye to his friends in the old neighborhood when he was 8. Mr. Young had graduated from law school and was now a lawyer. He was employed by a company that asked him to work in New York City.

In New York, the Youngs looked for a neighborhood like the one they had lived in in Salt Lake City. Mr. and Mrs.

the ball over the goalposts from the 3-yard line.) No one in the country had a higher extra-point kicking average than Mr. Young did.

During his senior year of college, Mr. Young played fullback for the BYU Cougars. (A fullback can run with the ball, catch passes, or block.) Mr. Young lived up to his nickname, "Grit." He gritted his teeth and looked tough on the football field. He was determined to run for a touchdown, and run he did.

In Mr. Young's senior year, he was the Cougars' rushing leader, with 423 yards. Years later, Steve laughed when he heard about his dad's yardage. At BYU, he would pass or run for close to that many yards in a single game!

After graduating from BYU and getting married, Mr. Young began law school at the University of Utah. Steve was born while his father was a student in the law school.

Mr. Young wasn't surprised that Steve became an athlete. Steve did push-ups at age 2. He dribbled a basketball at 3. He was well-coordinated and was always carrying some sort of ball.

Steve's brother Mike was born on Steve's second birthday. The two boys played together. Their play-group grew to include their sister Melissa, who was born when Steve was 4.

Steve was left-handed. Mr. Young tried to teach Steve how to throw with this right hand, and then changed his mind. "It didn't take him too long to figure out that

GROWING UP YOUNG

Jon Steven Young was born on October 11, 1961, in Salt Lake City, Utah. His parents, LeGrande and Sherry Young, called him by his middle name. People teased Mr. Young when Steve reached adulthood and became a famous football player. They said Mr. Young must have tucked a football into Steve's hospital crib.

Mr. Young laughed and said he hadn't. He waited a whole year or two before he taught Steve how to throw his first pass!

Although Steve was the Young's first son, he obviously wasn't named after his father. Instead, the Youngs picked the name because they thought it sounded businesslike. Little did they know what business he would go into!

Mr. and Mrs. Young met while students at Brigham Young University, in Provo, Utah, about 40 miles southeast of Salt Lake City. The university is named after Mr. Young's great-great grandfather. During his sophomore year at BYU, Mr. Young was an extra-point kicker. (After a team scores a touchdown, it gets an extra point if it succeeds in kicking

Steve had wanted the approval of the San Francisco fans.

Steve's father, LeGrande, said that Steve "just wants to please people. He can't stand someone not liking him."

For many years, the San Francisco fans hadn't liked Steve. They preferred the former starting quarterback, Joe Montana. Joe had led San Francisco to four conference championships and four Super Bowl wins.

Steve had been Joe's backup for four years. Then, in 1991, Steve became the 49ers' starting quarterback. Steve's feelings were hurt when he heard people complain that he wasn't Joe Montana. But Steve knew that what those people said was true. He had not been able to win important games like the NFC championship.

Now he had! As Steve kept on running around the field after the game, he began hearing a different stadium cheer. "MVP! MVP! MVP!" Steve was overcome with joy. He looked into the stands and punched his fist into the air.

Steve was thrilled. He spoke to reporters after the game. "This is one of the greatest feelings of all time," Steve said. "I wish anybody who ever played the game could feel it."

Two weeks later, Steve helped the 49ers beat San Diego at the Super Bowl. He threw six touchdowns, a Super Bowl record. He won the Most Valuable Player award. He showed the world that he was the best quarterback in the NFL that season. Maybe even one of the best ever.

There would be no "three-peat" for them.

The 49ers' pass protectors had guarded Steve well during the game. "We didn't want [Dallas] battering Steve," San Francisco tight end Brent Jones said.

Steve completed almost half of his 29 passes, and he did not throw one interception.

Troy, on the other hand, had been under a lot of pressure. The Dallas offensive line wasn't able to protect him as well as it had in the past. Troy was sacked four times and knocked down 19 times after he threw the ball. He threw three interceptions. Despite all the trouble he had, though, Troy completed 30 of 53 passes, for 380 yards. That was an NFC Championship Game record.

Unlike Troy, Steve didn't break any records, but he finally won the NFC championship. Up in the stands, a fan waved a sign. It said STEVE YOUNG CAN DO IT ALL! Maybe Steve could win the Super Bowl, too!

At the end of the game, the two mud-caked quarterbacks met in the middle of the field. "I'm happy for you," Troy said, graciously extending his hand to Steve. "Good luck against San Diego."

It was a painful moment for Troy, but a happy one for Steve. Steve cradled the winning football in his left arm, the one he throws with, and took off on a victory run. The fans were hoarse and cheering Steve on. "Steve! Steve! Steve!"

Was the crowd really cheering for him? This was a dream come true! Ever since he joined the 49ers, in 1987,

Whumpf! Steve's pass hit Ricky full-force in the stomach. Ricky held onto the ball and slipped past the slower Dallas linebackers. He outran them down the muddy field for 29 yards and dove into the right corner of the end zone to complete the play. Touchdown! The roar from the crowd was deafening.

A few minutes later, 49er fullback William Floyd scored on a one-yard run. Steve could hardly believe it. Just 7 1/2 minutes had passed, and his team was up, 21–0!

The San Francisco fans went wild, but Steve stayed calm. He knew he had to focus on playing well. Dallas could come back.

Dallas did. The Cowboys scored twice that first half. Then, with just eight seconds left in the half, Steve lobbed a high pass toward Jerry Rice. It was a 28-yard bull's-eye! Jerry leaped up and grabbed it in the lefthand corner of the end zone. He hit the ground and held on tight to give the 49ers a 31–14 halftime lead!

That was "really the play of the game," Steve said later. After that, he began to relax. He felt as if he were in total control of the game.

Midway through the third quarter, Steve broke to the outside and ran with the ball. He dove over Dallas safety James Washington and touched the ball down inside the goal line. San Francisco now led 38–21!

In the end, the scoreboard told the story: San Francisco had won, 38–28. The Cowboys were stunned.

8 STEVE YOUNG

They leaped up out of their seats in a frenzy of cheering, clapping, and waving. The Niners were leading, 7–0.

After regaining possession of the ball, Dallas fumbled. Things were going well for the 49ers. The Cowboys weren't making things as tough as they had earlier in the season.

When a little more than four minutes had passed, Steve took charge of the 49ers' first offensive drive. He took the snap from San Francisco center Bart Oates. Steve dropped back and quickly studied the Dallas defense. San Francisco wide receivers Jerry Rice and John Taylor were covered by Dallas defenders. Running back Ricky Watters was well guarded, too, but Steve thought there was a chance he could get through. Steve pumped his throwing arm as if he were going straight ahead to Jerry, and then pumped again and threw to Ricky instead.

HEAD TO HEAD

The NFL compares its quarterbacks each season by a number rating that is called the "quarterback rating." That number is determined by four things that the quarterback does that season: 1) how often he throws a touchdown pass 2) how often he throws an interception 3) the average number of passes he completes and 4) the number of yards he averages on each throw.

the conference championship game. Troy and the Cowboys had done the same thing the year before, in 1993! Steve was the losing quarterback each time, and it bothered him.

"It weighs on me as a part of this team," Steve told Ira Miller of the *San Francisco Chronicle*. The San Francisco fans complained that Steve was not able to win important games like this.

The fact was, Steve was 33 years old and one of the best quarterbacks in NFL history. Steve had earned the highest rating *(see box on page 7)* of any NFL quarterback four years in a row. No other quarterback had been rated first so many years in a row.

Steve was very good at what he did. He could throw a pass so that a receiver could catch it easily. And he could run! Steve could tuck the ball under his arm, break away from his opponents, and dive over the goal line into the end zone.

Today, Steve needed to use all of his talents. Otherwise, the Niners would not be going to the Super Bowl.

Steve had guided the 49ers to a victory over Dallas earlier in the season. By throwing two touchdowns and running for another, he helped the Niners beat the Cowboys, 21–14. Steve needed to beat Dallas one more time.

In the first quarter, Steve watched San Francisco defensive back Eric Davis score the first touchdown. Eric intercepted a pass that Troy had thrown. Eric then ran 44 yards for the touchdown.

The interception drove San Francisco fans crazy.

GOING TO THE BIG ONE

Steve Young looked up at the screaming fans who filled San Francisco's Candlestick Park. Steve was the San Francisco 49ers' starting quarterback. It was January 15, 1995, and the 49ers were getting ready to play the Dallas Cowboys in the National Football Conference (NFC) Championship Game. Many people believed that San Francisco and Dallas were the two best teams in the National Football League. No doubt, this championship would be exciting. Winning it meant a trip to the Big One — the Super Bowl!

The San Francisco fans were standing, waving, and cheering. The fans rarely cheered for Steve, even though he had been playing for the 49ers for eight years. Maybe they would cheer for him today!

Steve looked out onto the field at Dallas's quarterback, Troy Aikman. Troy had done something Steve had not — win the NFC championship and the Super Bowl that followed. In fact, in 1994, it had been Troy and the Cowboys who kept the 49ers out of the Super Bowl by beating them in

CONTENTS

1 Going to the Big One.................... 6

2 Growing Up Young..................... 12

3 Rushing Through High School........... 20

4 Waiting in the Wings................... 27

5 A Different Path to the Pros............. 36

6 In Joe's Shadow....................... 44

7 Out of the Shadow..................... 53

8 A Dream Come True................... 59

   Steve Young's Career Stats.............. 64

To my children —
Andy, Robbie, and Laura —
and to young athletes everywhere.
Like Steve Young, you may not be the best player
on your team today,
but you can be the best tomorrow.
Hang in there!

And to my editor, Margaret Sieck,
with gratitude.

HEAD TO HEAD FOOTBALL

STEVE YOUNG

by Darice Bailer

A Sports Illustrated For Kids Book

TIMEOUT!

HEADS UP, FOOTBALL FANS

HEAD-TO-HEAD FOOTBALL is a unique book; it has two fronts and no back. It is somewhat like two football teams facing each other at the line of scrimmage! Choose the superstar you want to read about first, read his story, then flip the book over and read about the other player.

You'll read how two different players from two different backgrounds ended up in the National Football League. You'll see how they're alike, too. You'll get the lowdown on the San Francisco 49ers' record-setting quarterback, Steve Young, and the inside story of the Dallas Cowboys' Super Bowl-winning super quarterback, Troy Aikman.

After reading both athletes' stories, tackle the amazing center section of the book. It has fantastic photos, complete statistics, and a comic strip, all of which show just how these two quarterbacks stack up against each other.

Okay, it's time for the coin toss. So pick Steve or Troy, and get ready for all the Head-to-Head action!